Bird House
Coloring Book

PKJ Publishing

At PKJ Publishing (Peace, Kindness, Joy), our mission is to spread positivity and enhance well-being through the medium of coloring books. By merging intricate illustrations with a diverse range of themes, our aim is to empower individuals to explore their artistic potential, foster mindfulness, and experience the joy of bringing vibrant hues to life on every page. Our commitment is to provide a range of coloring books that not only entertain but also uplift spirits, allowing individuals of all ages to experience the therapeutic power of art while embracing the essence of imagination, one beautifully colored page at a time.

This book belongs to:

_____

Thank you for your purchase!
We hope you enjoy your journey of coloring and find the pages within the book delightful.

You may also like:

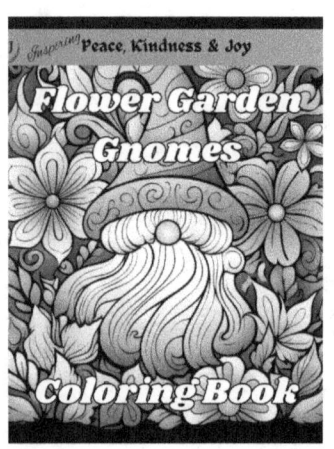 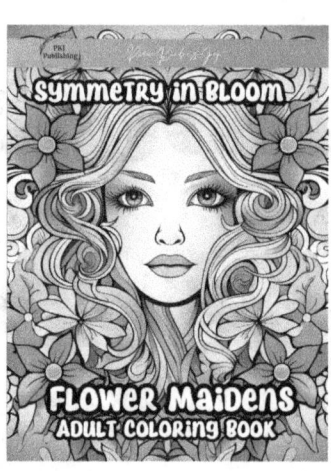 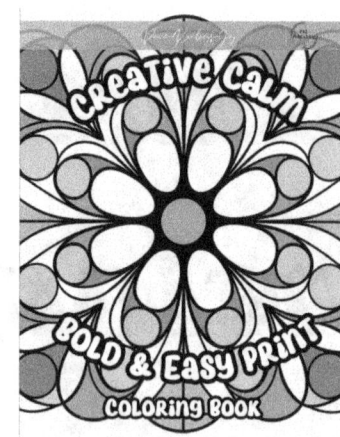 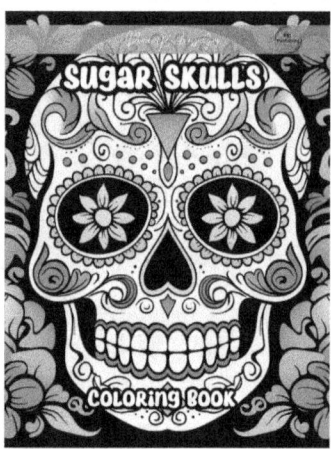

Be sure to share your beautiful creations on our Facebook page!

PKJ Facebook Page

PKJ Website

PKJ Amazon Books

PKJ Etsy Books

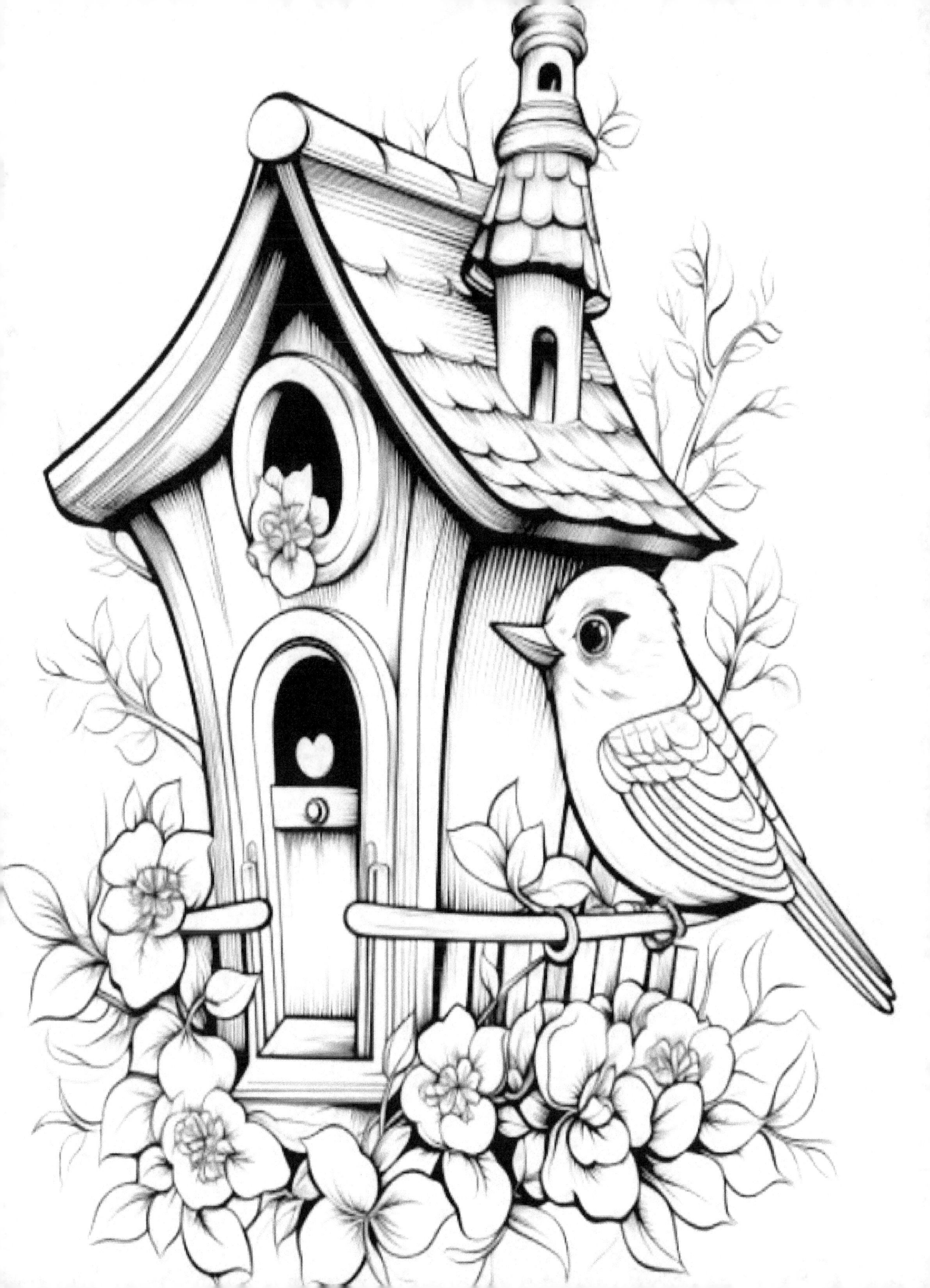

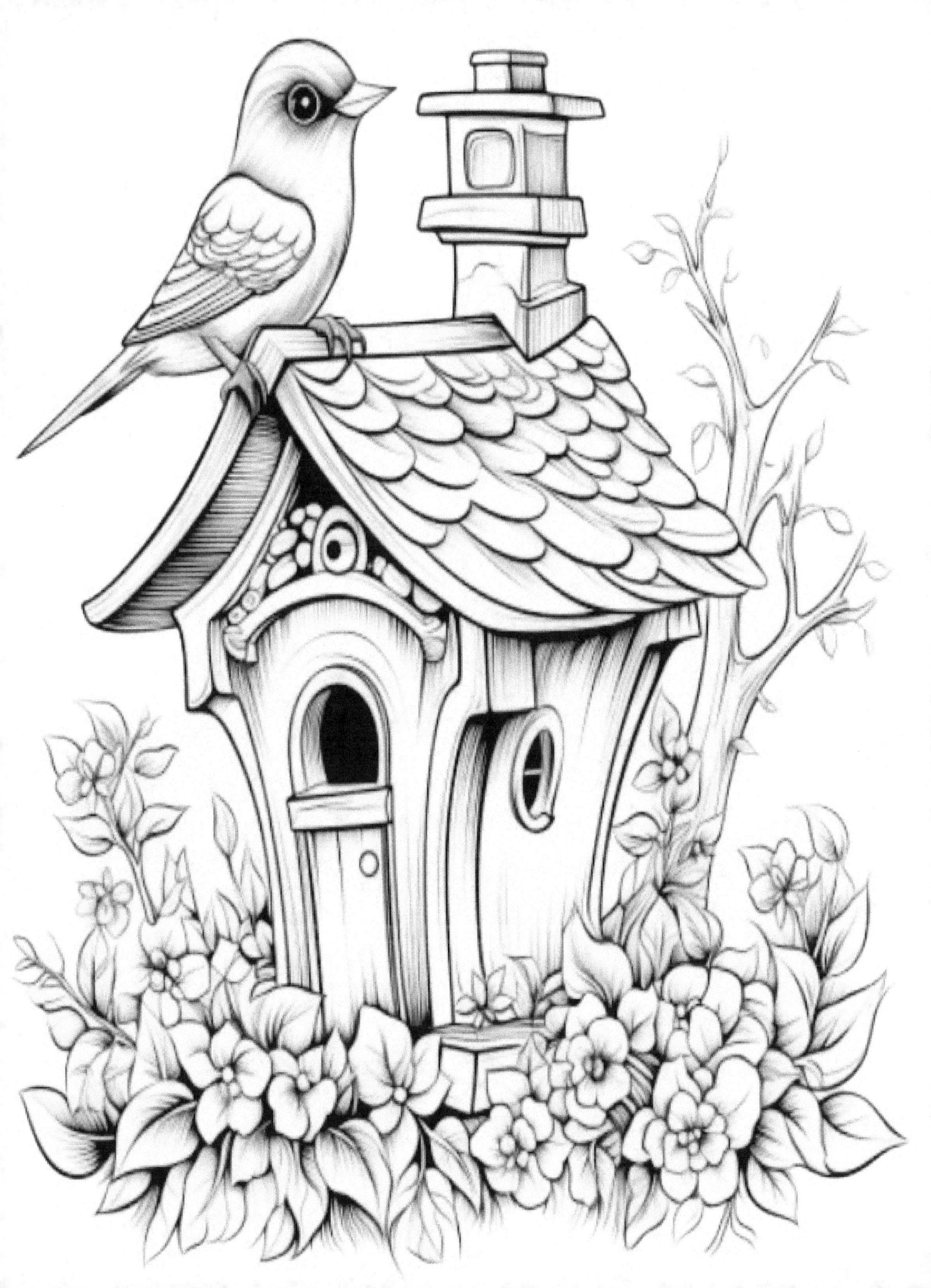

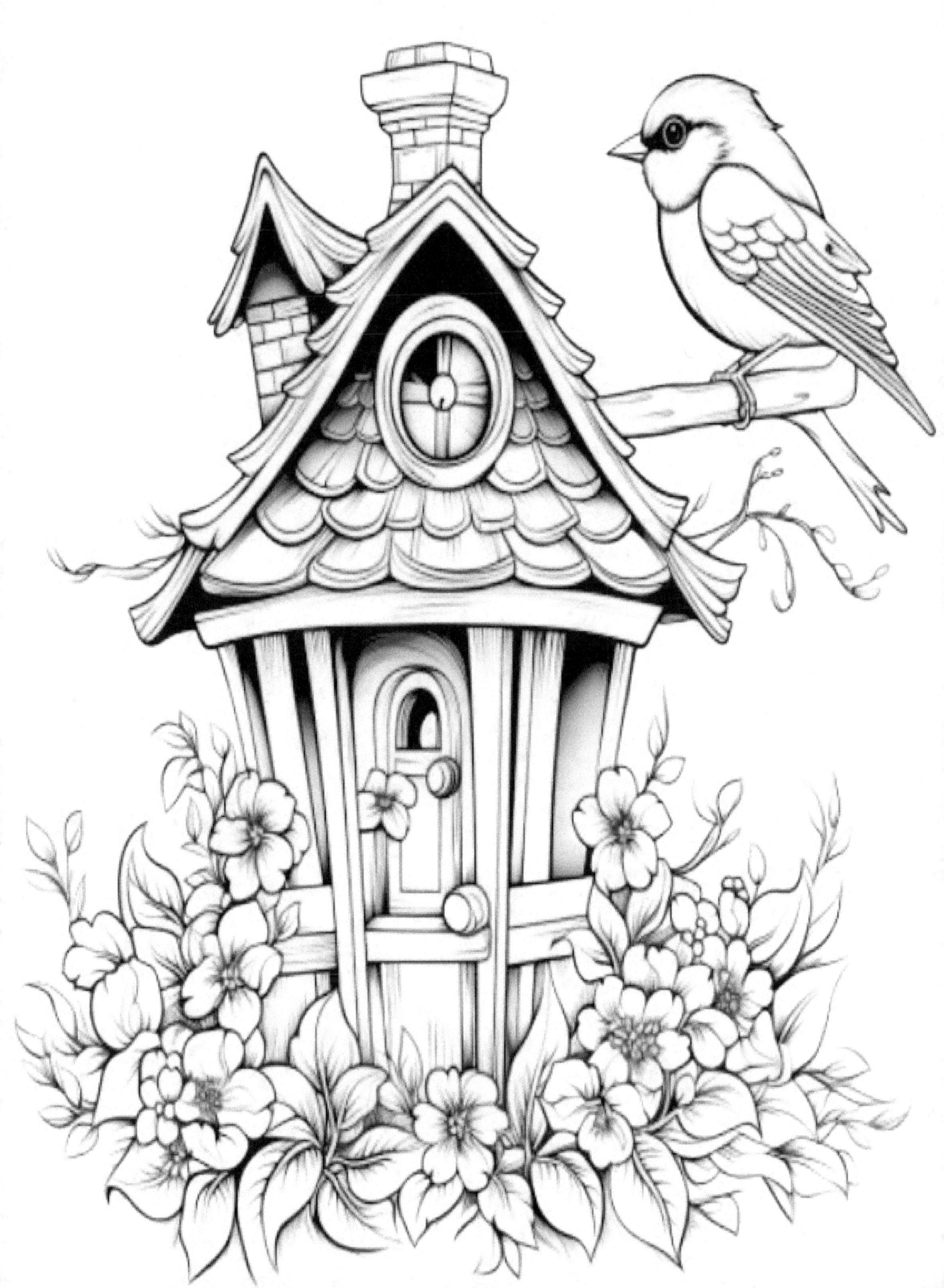

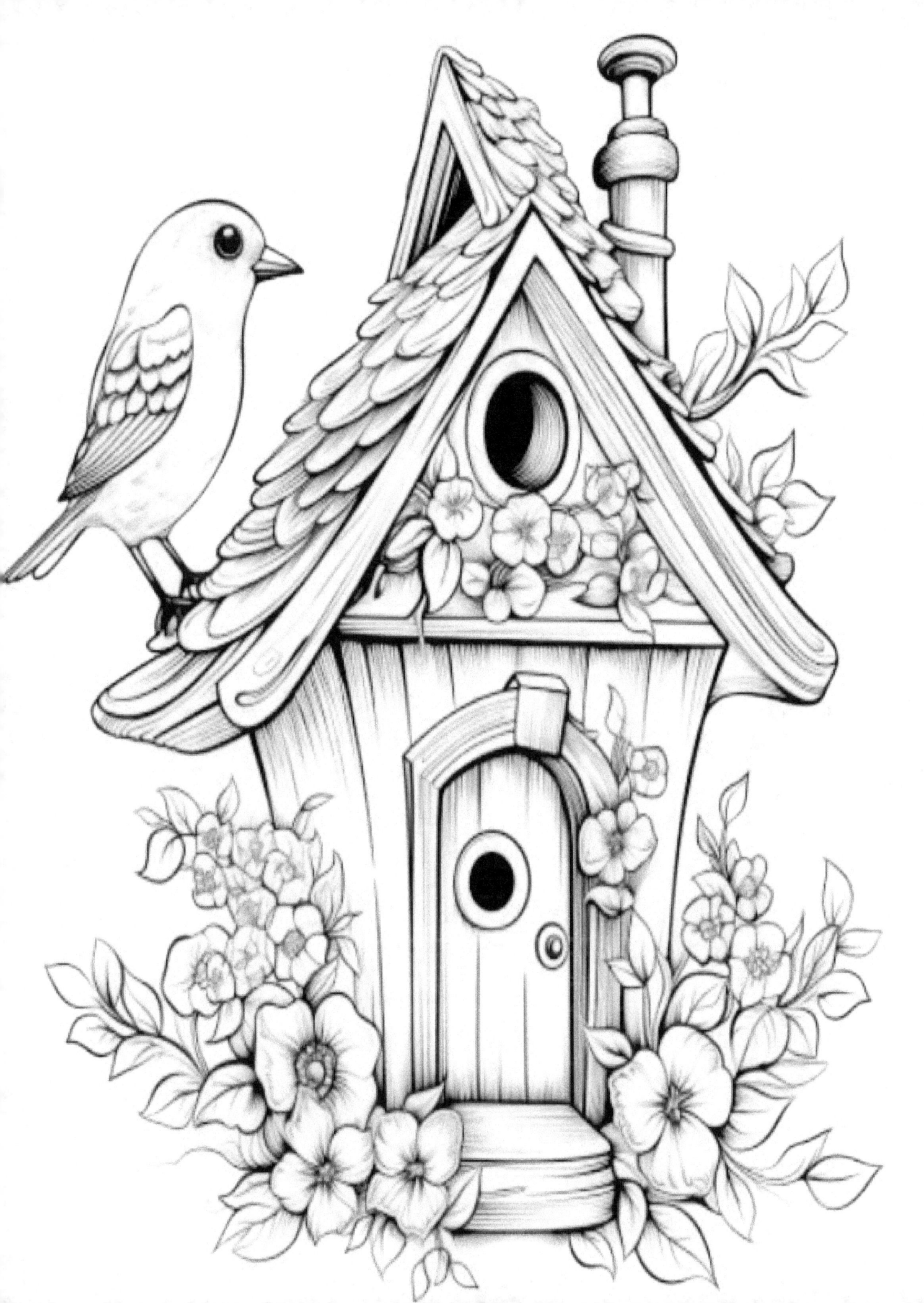

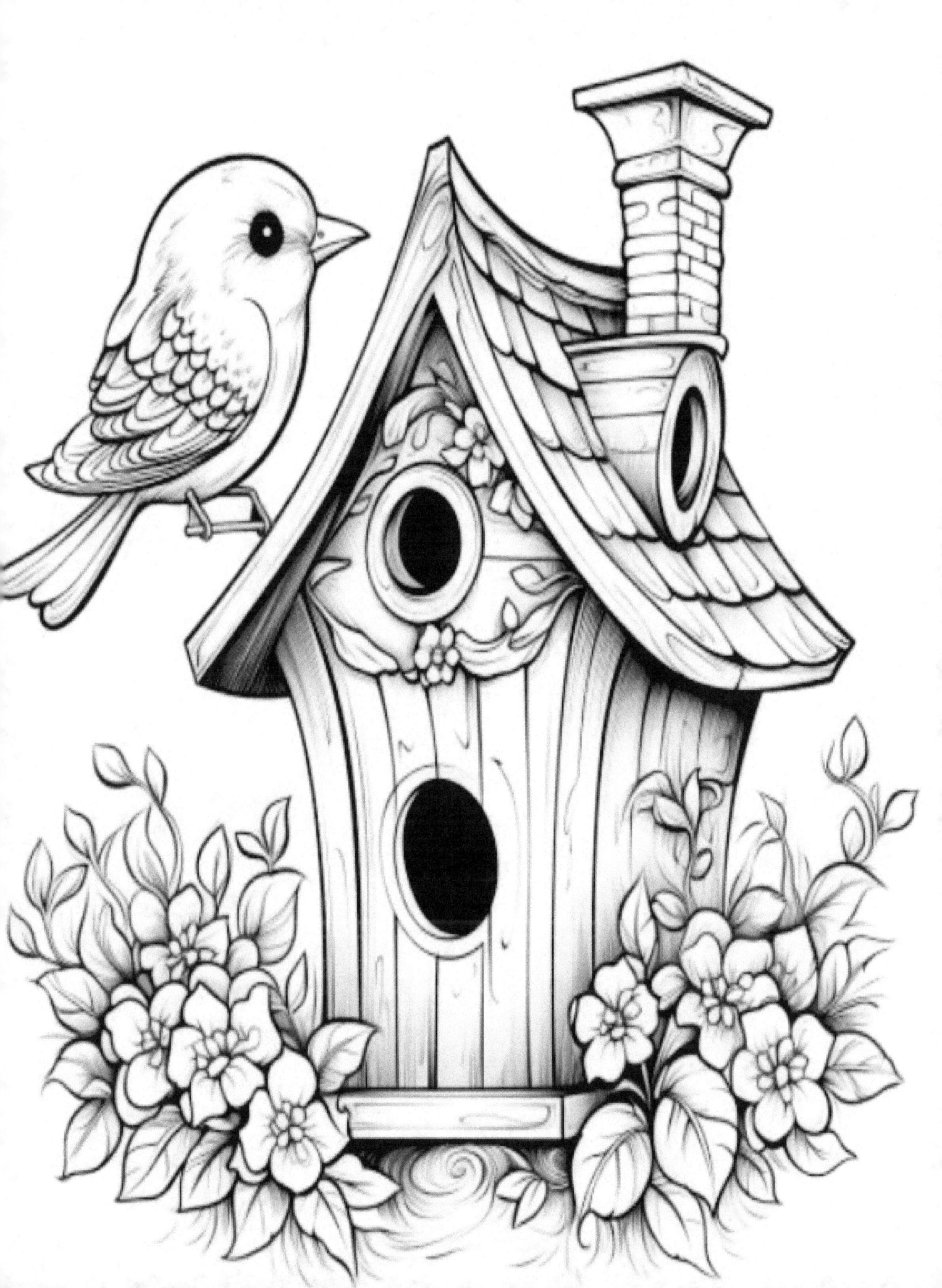

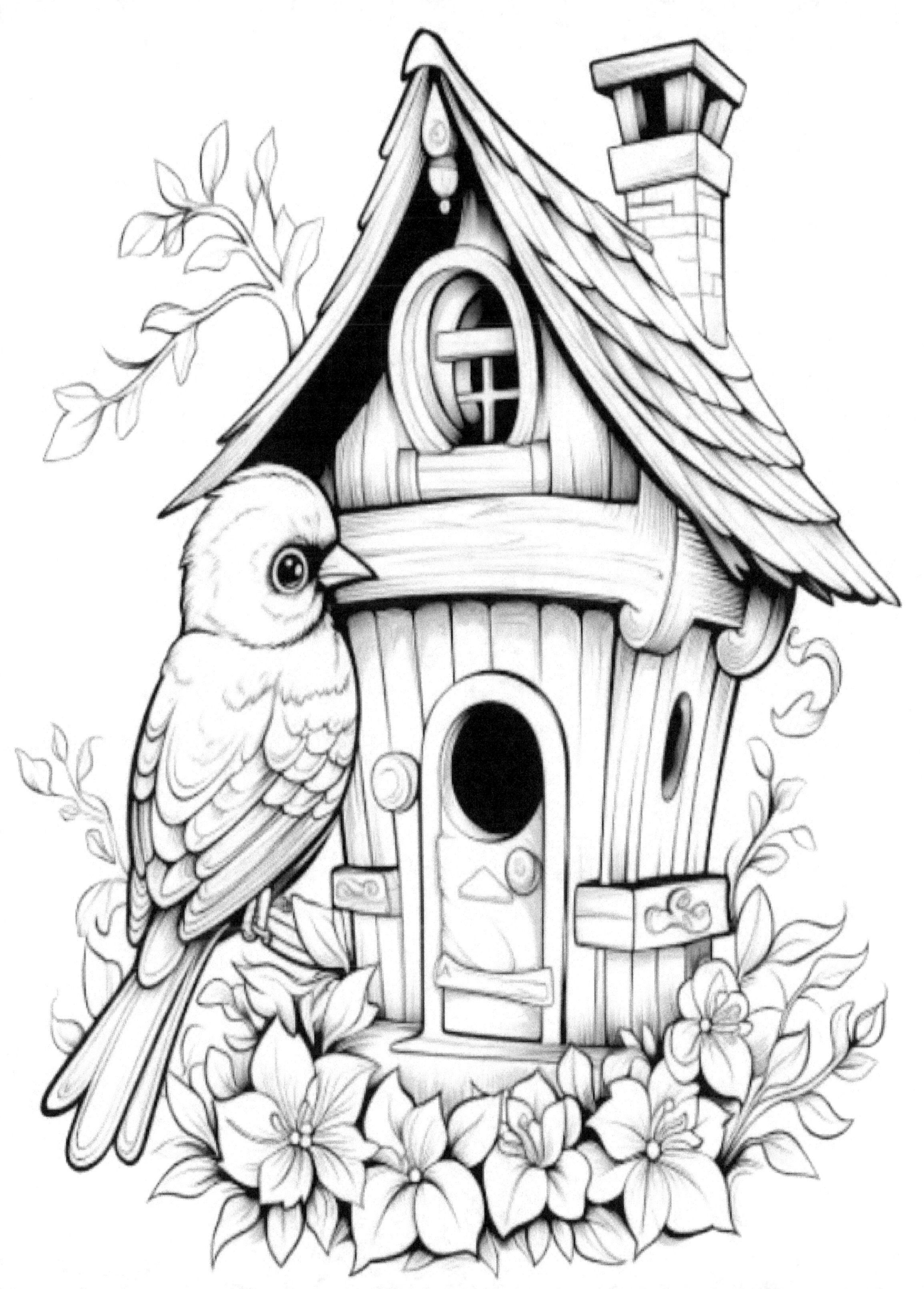

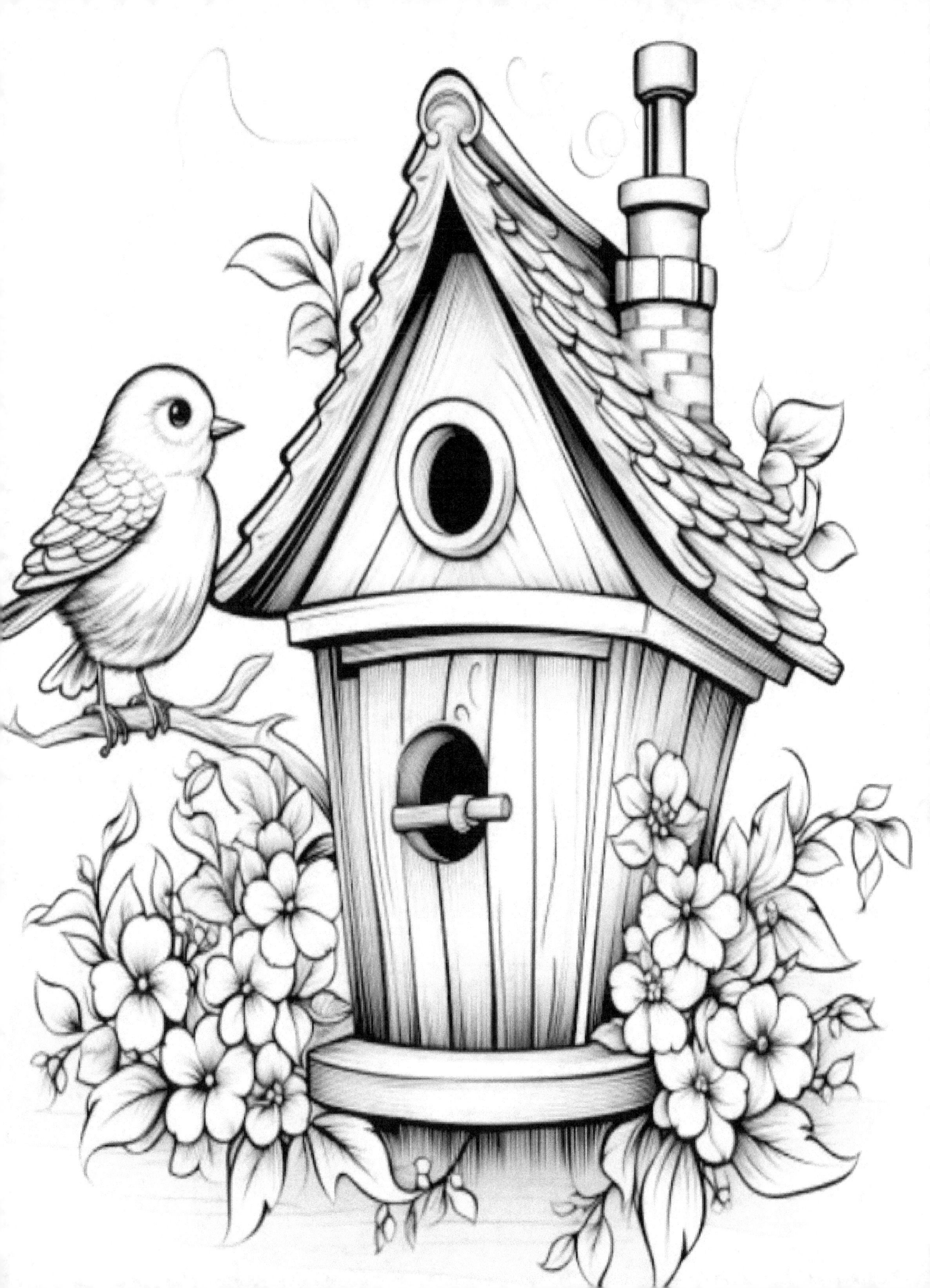

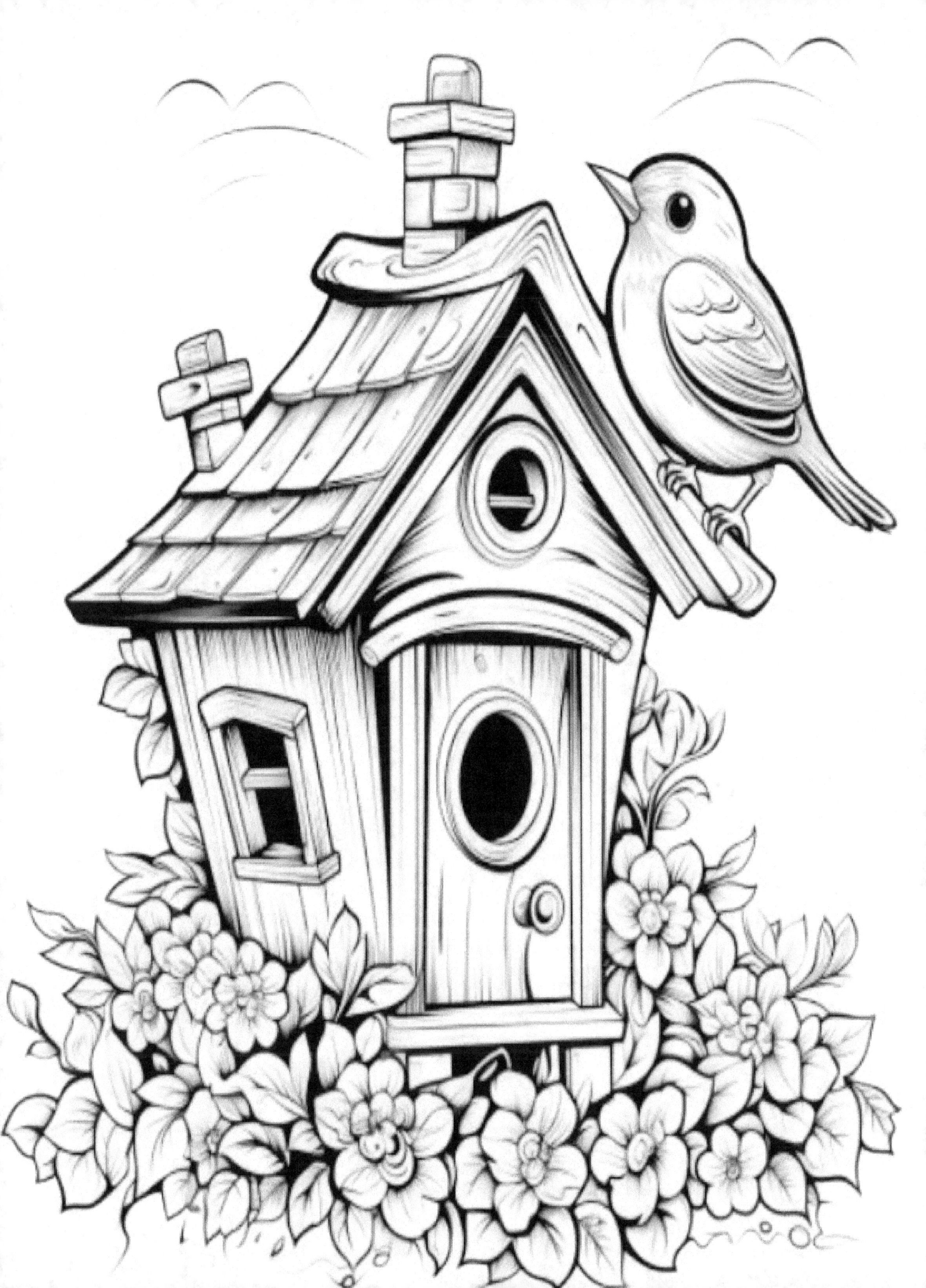

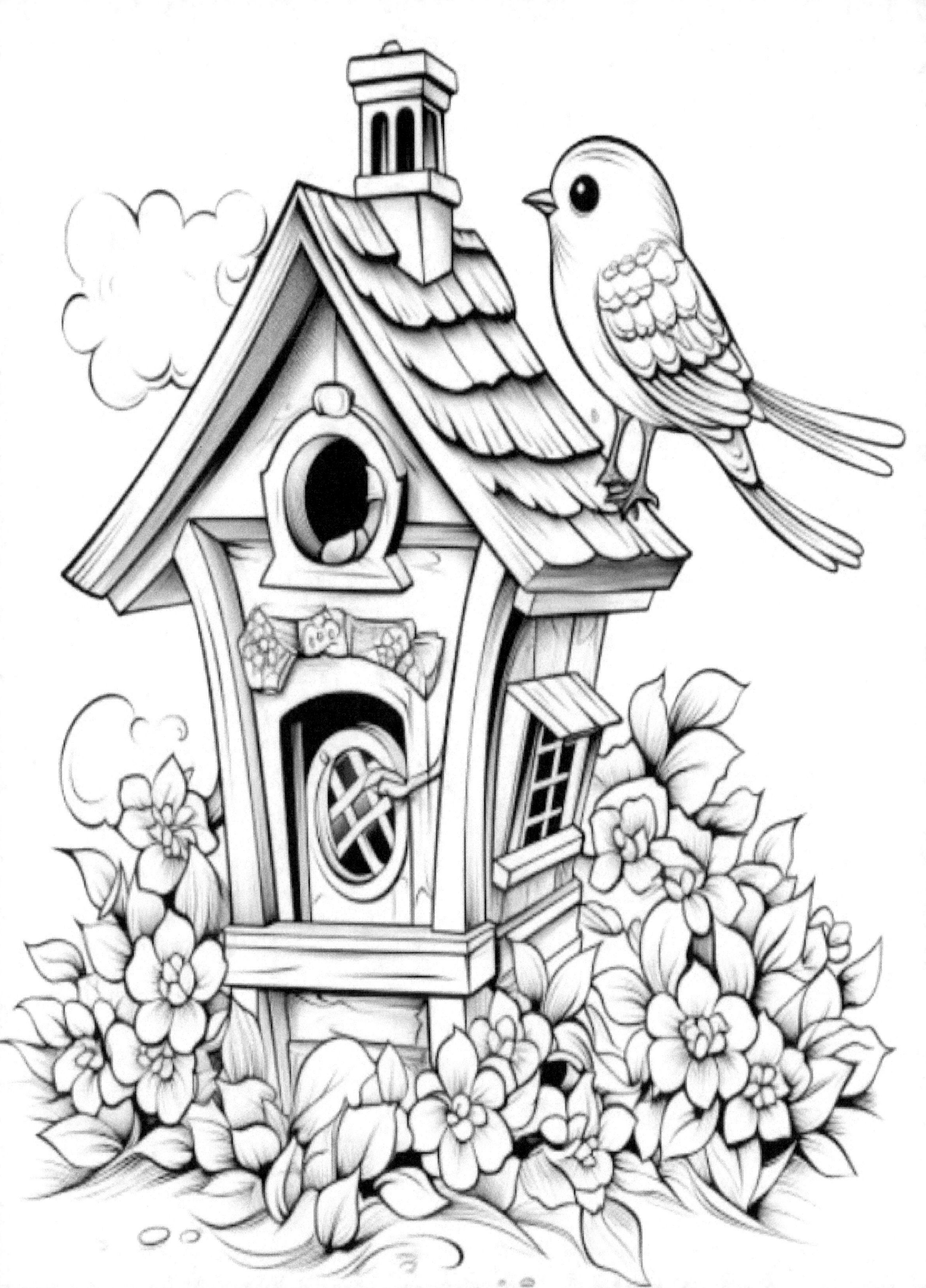

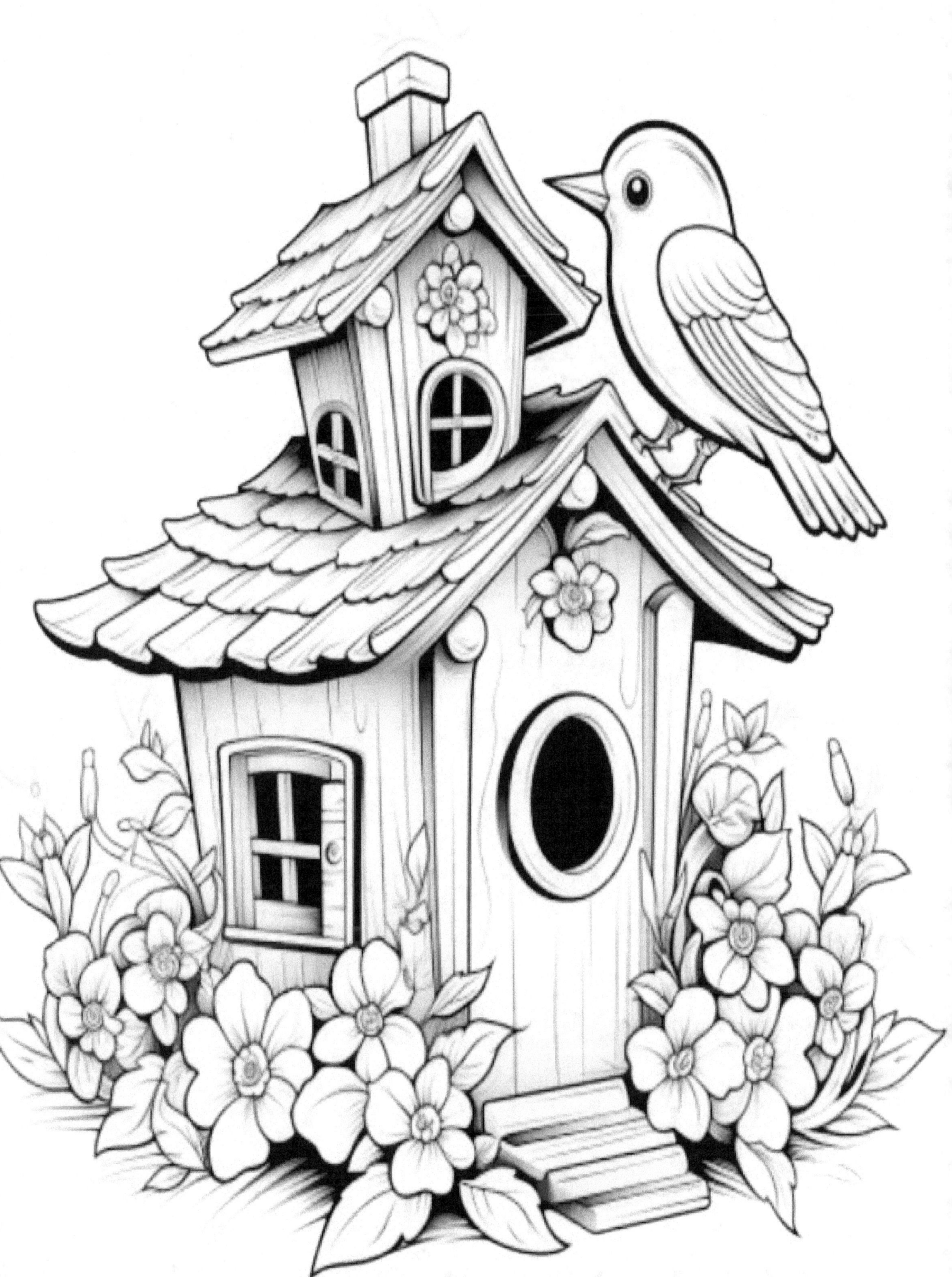

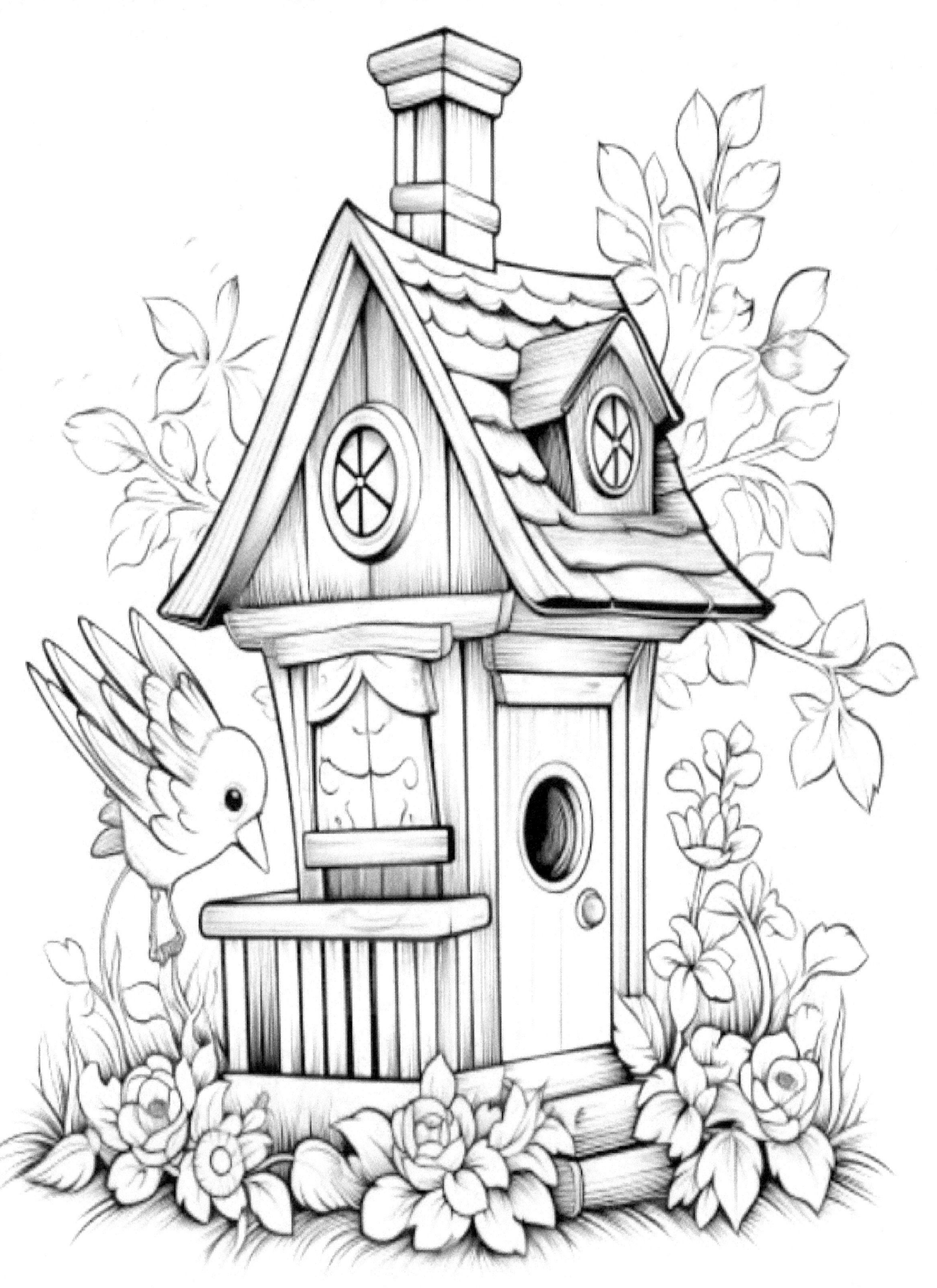

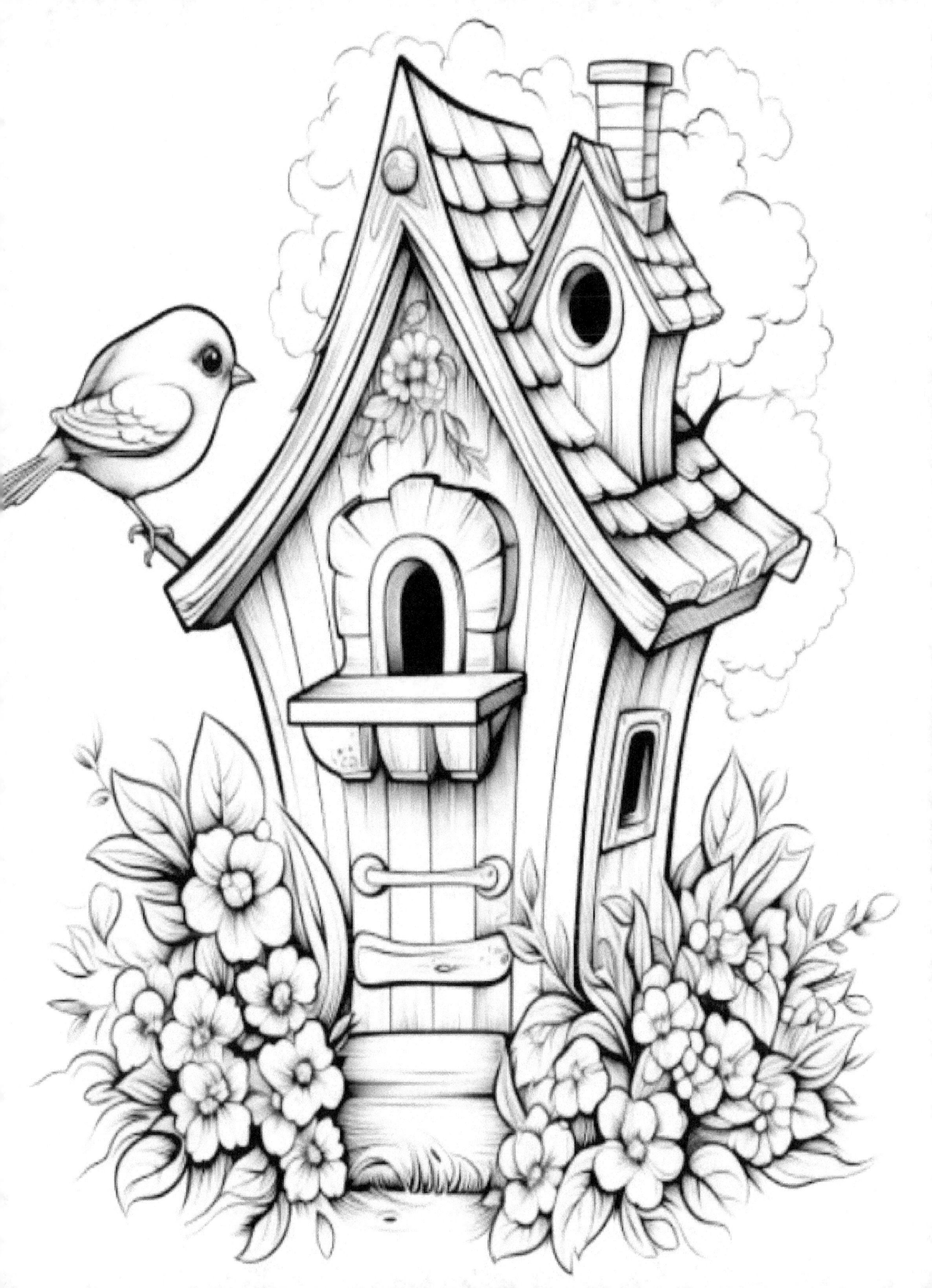

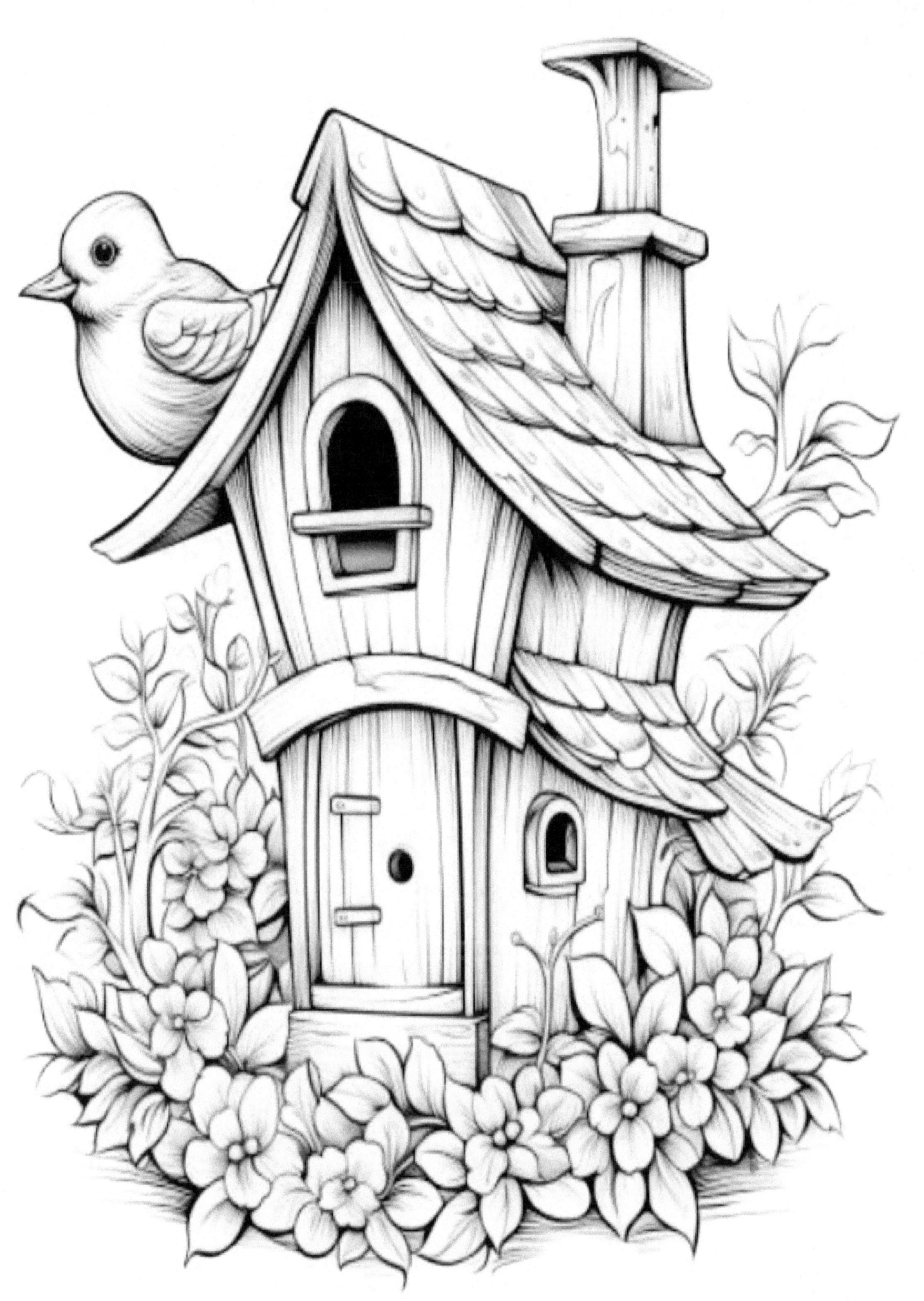

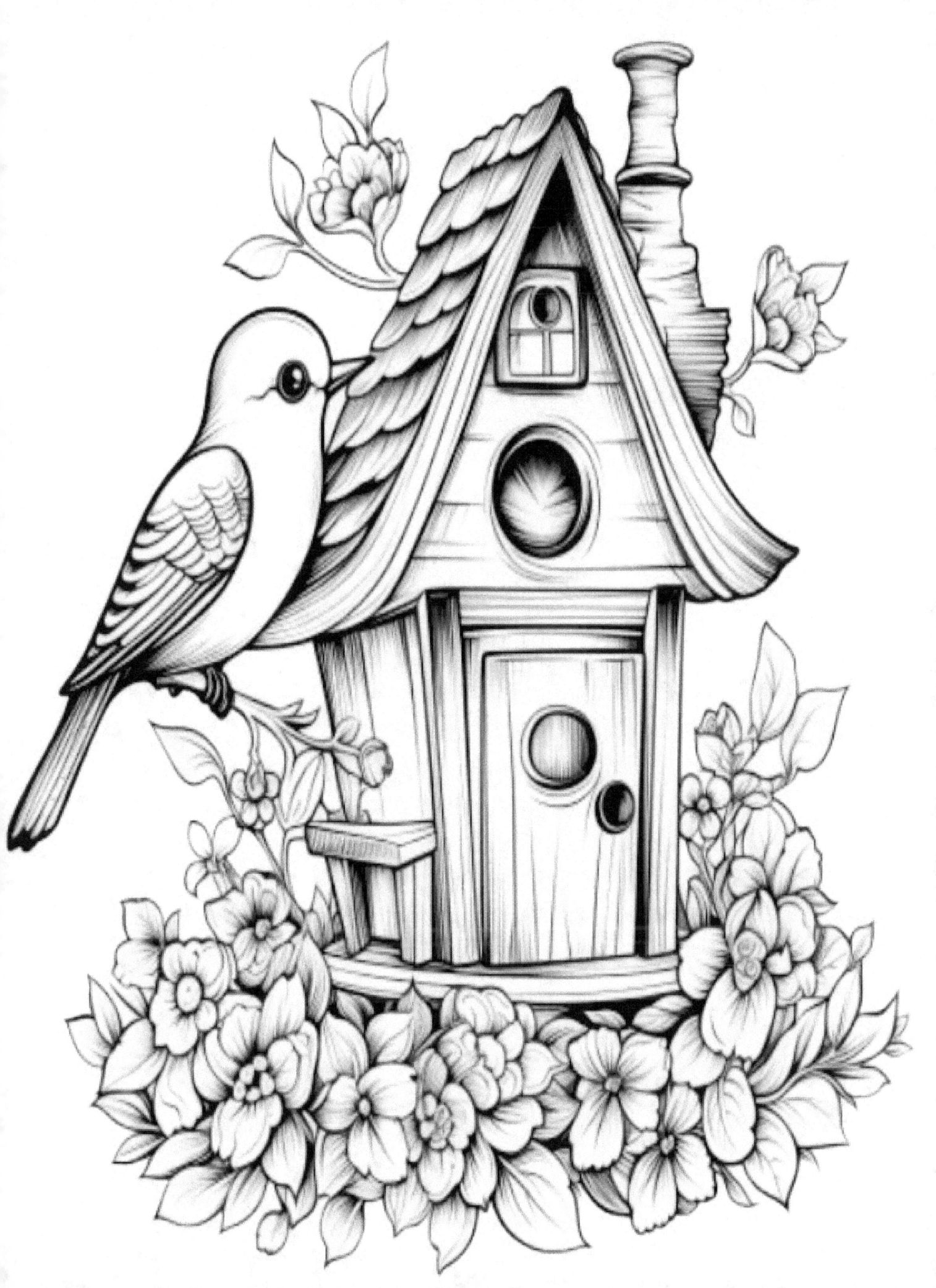

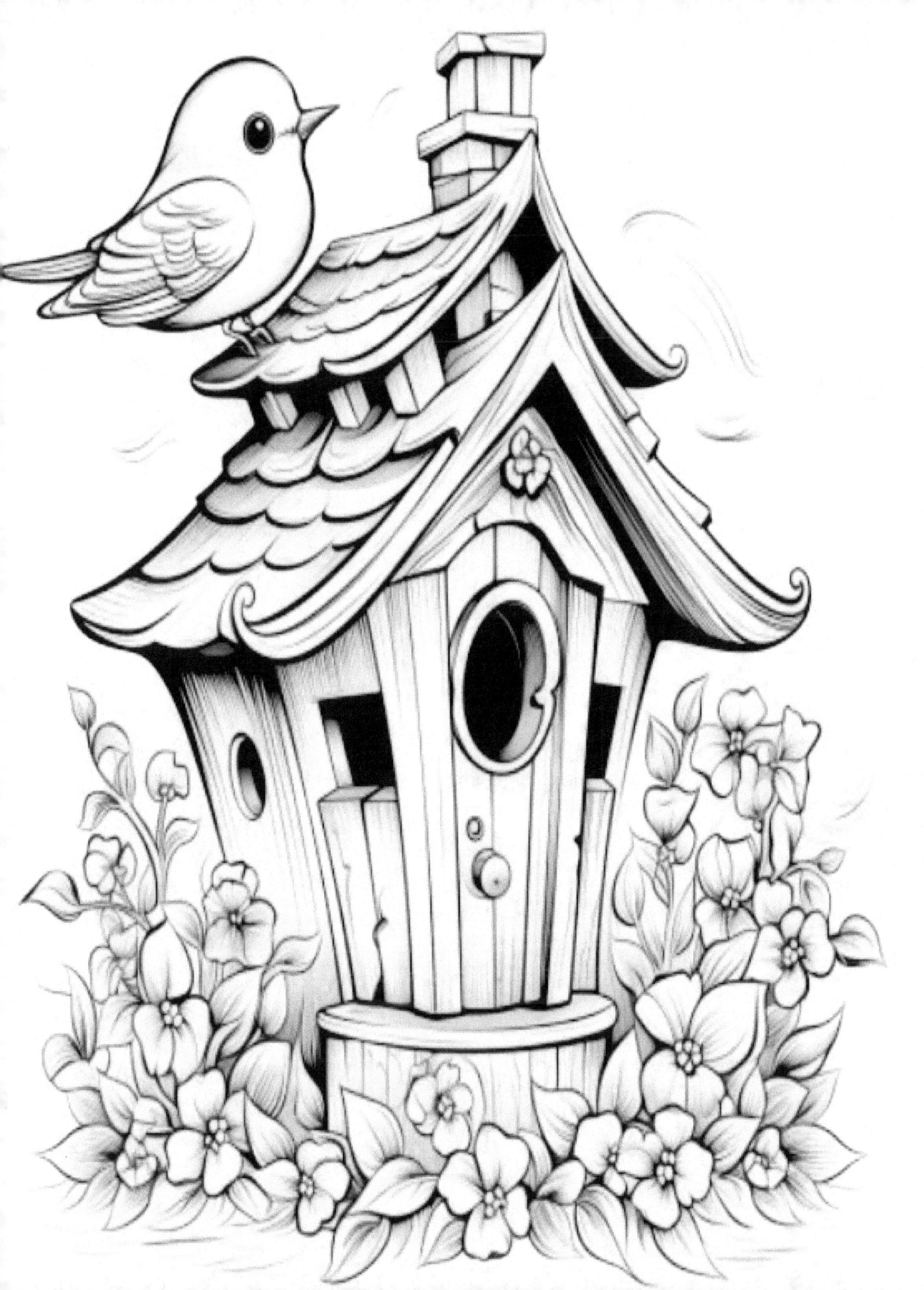

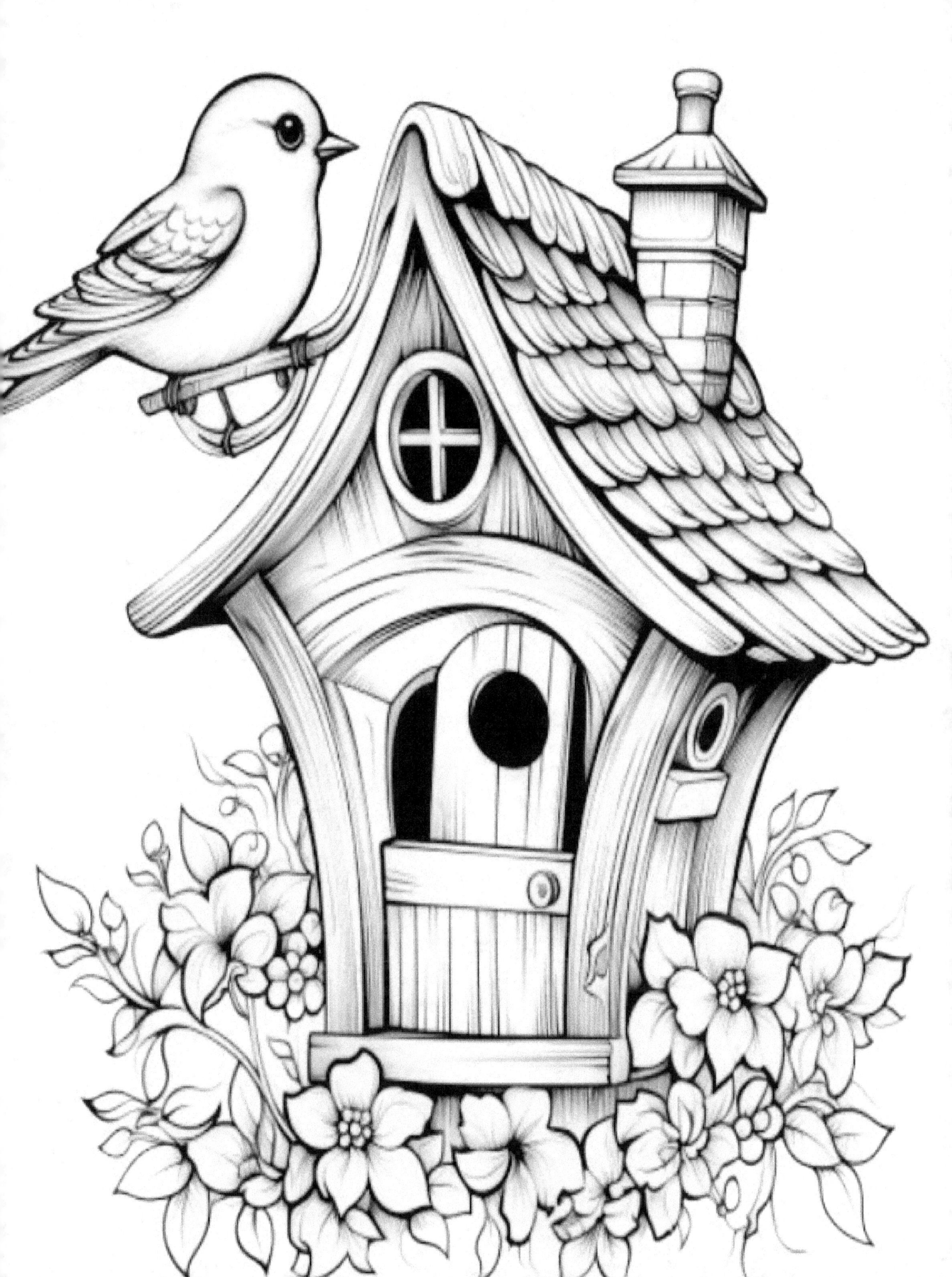

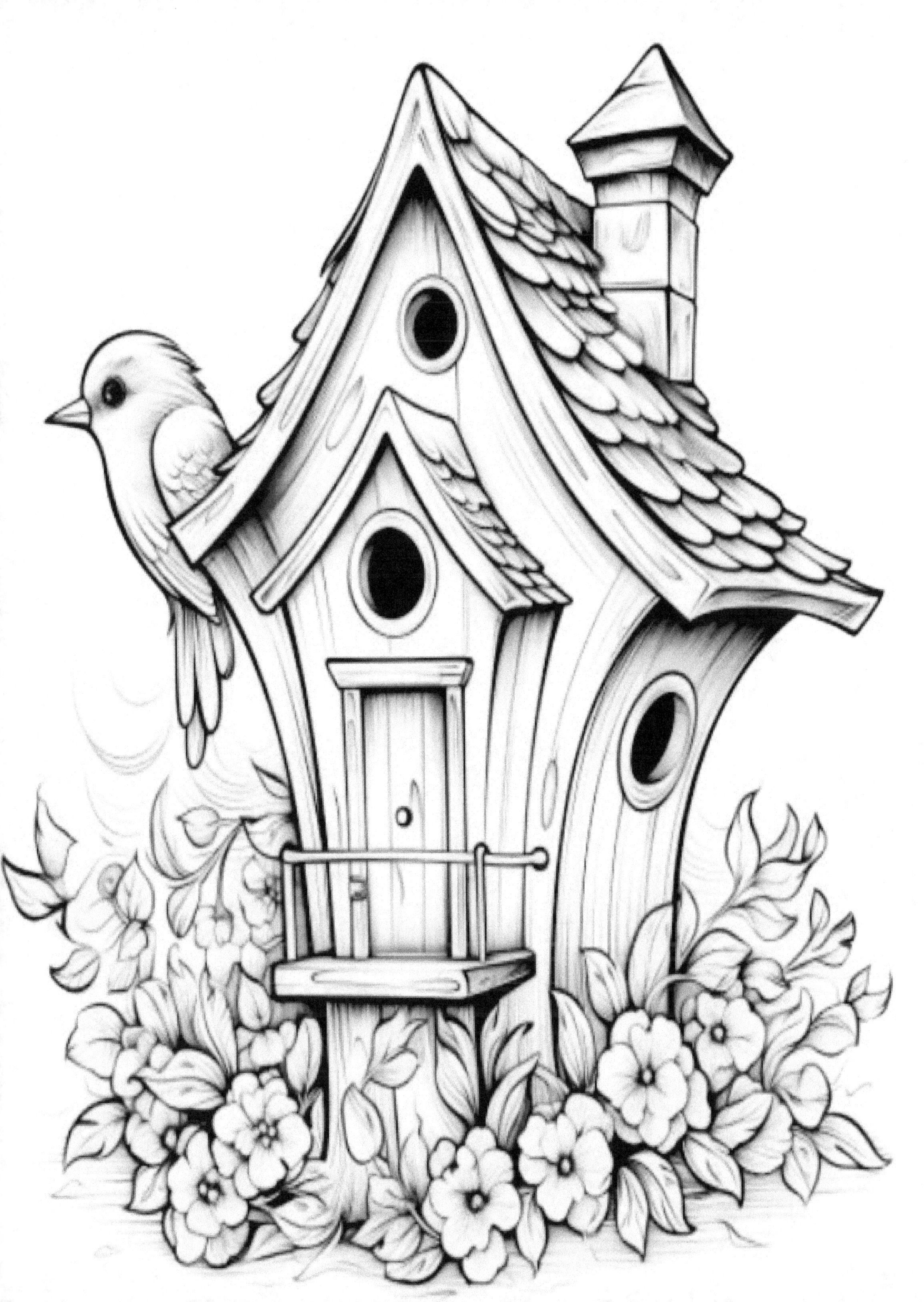

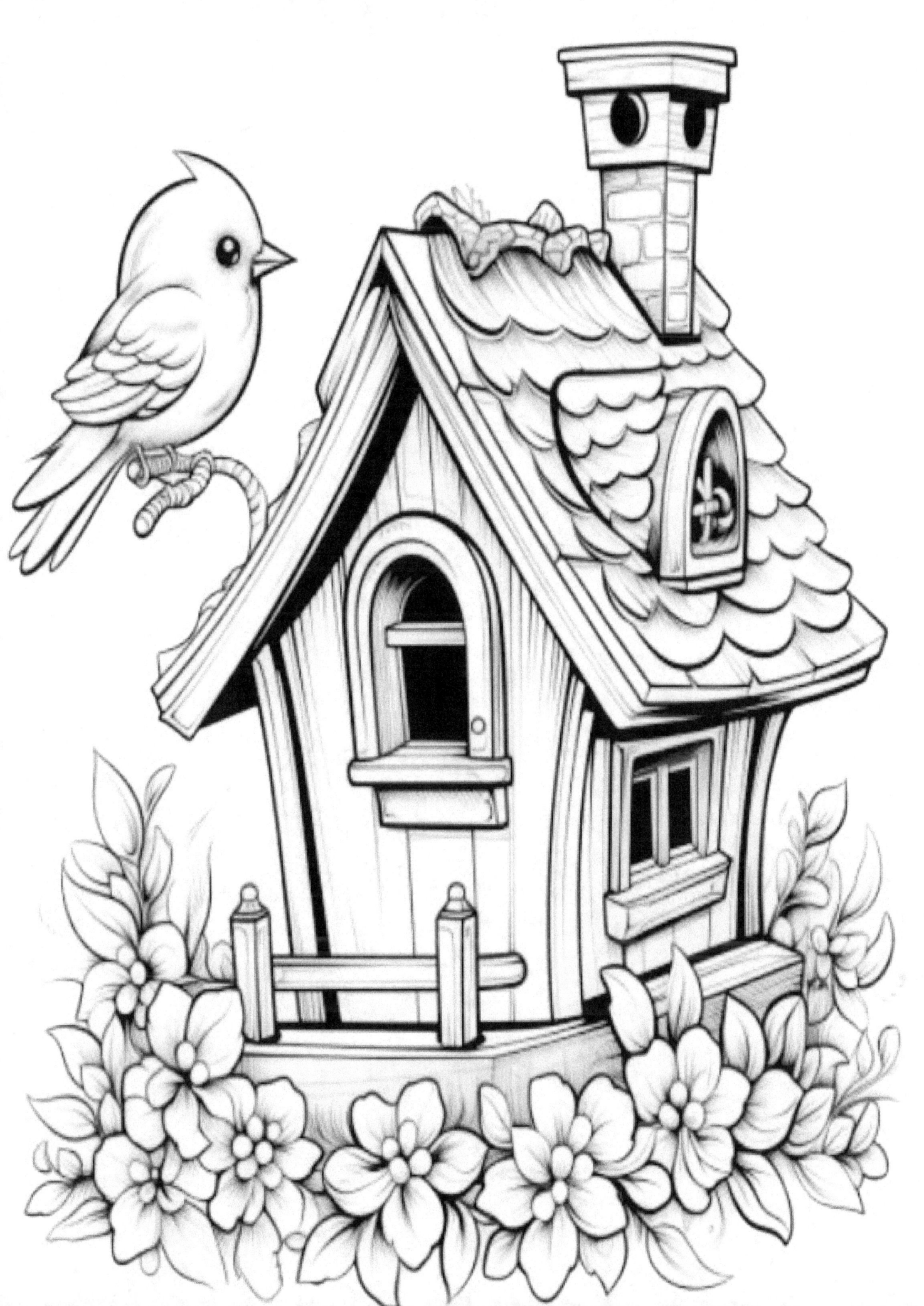

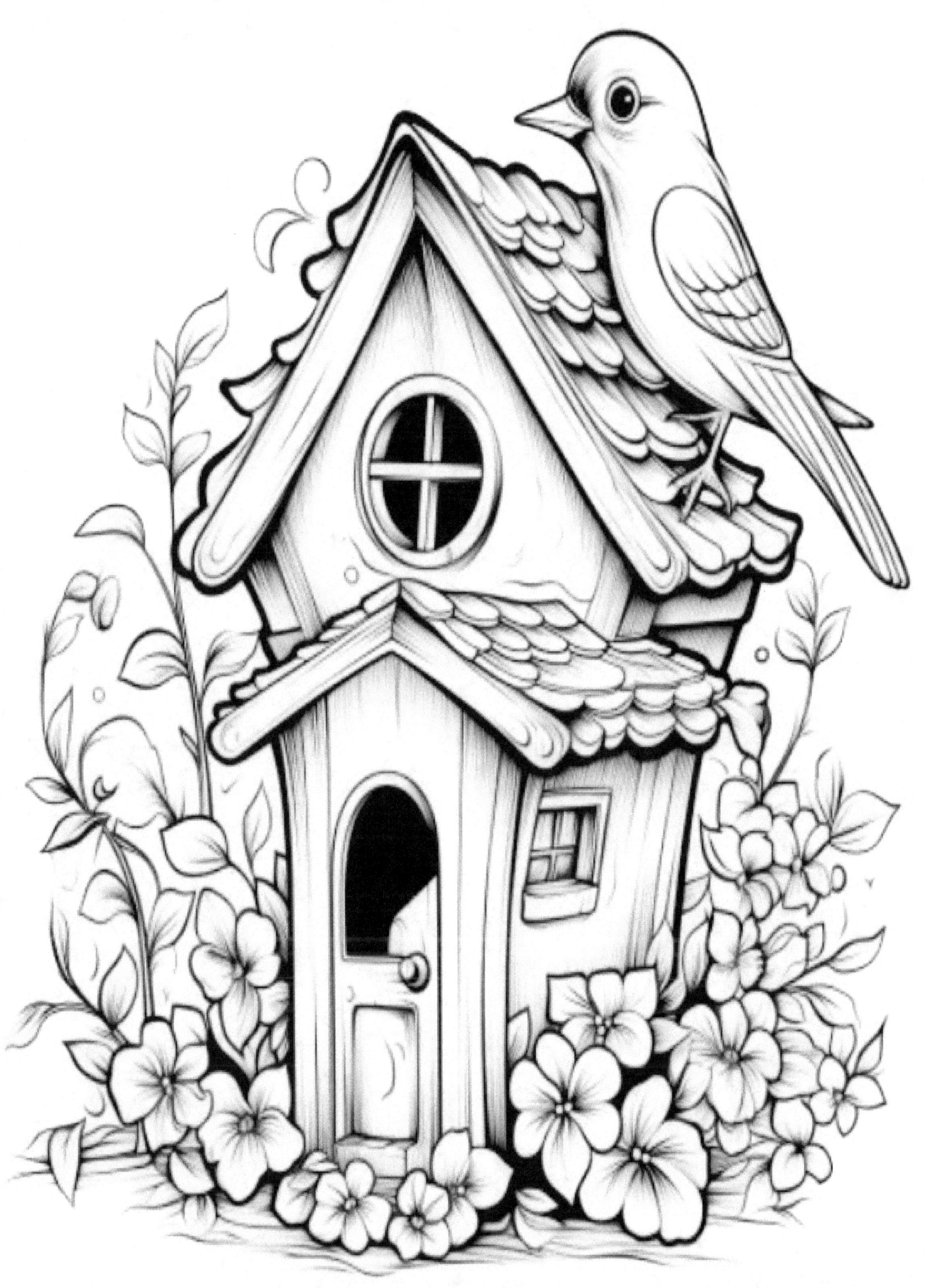

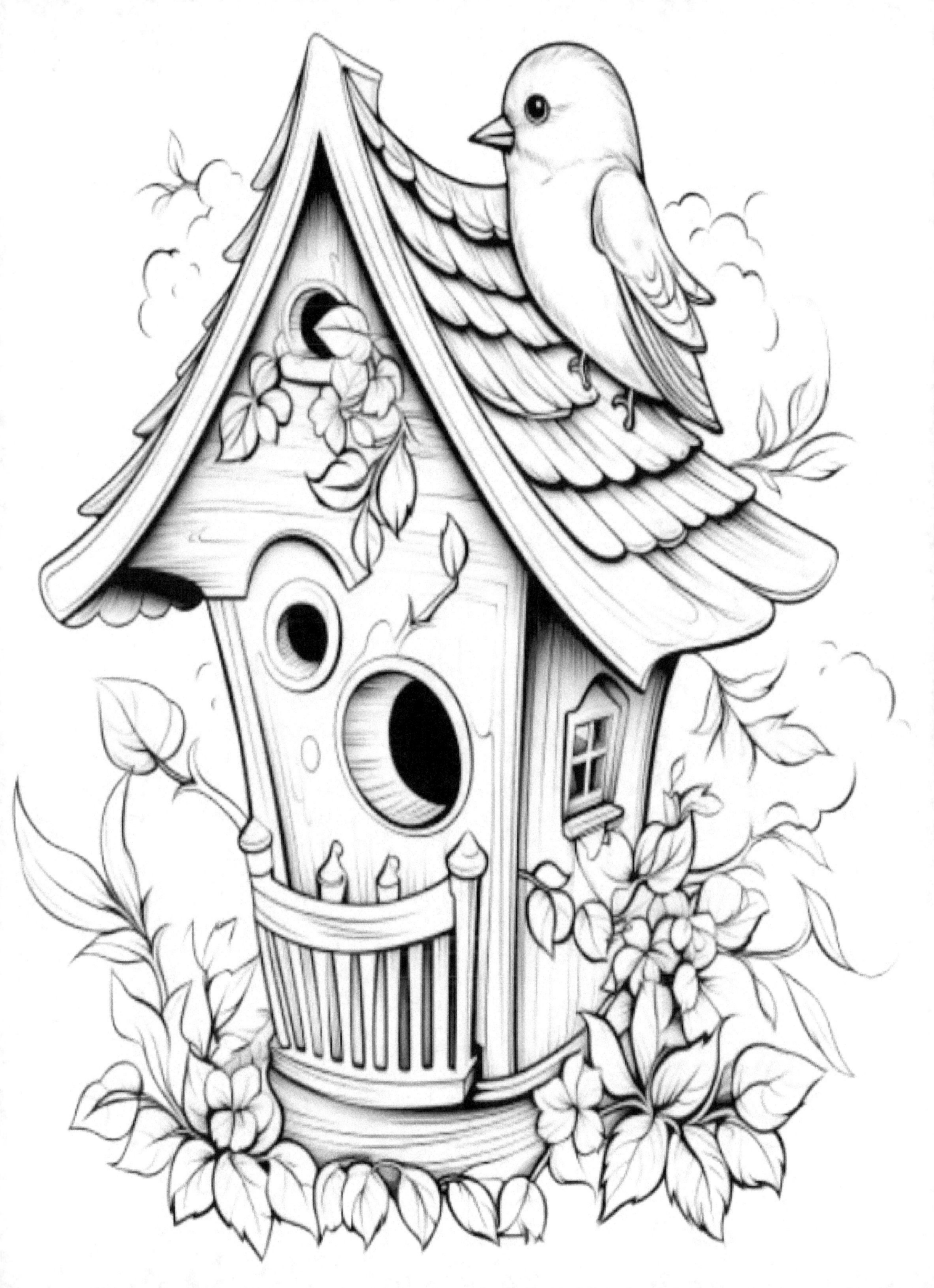

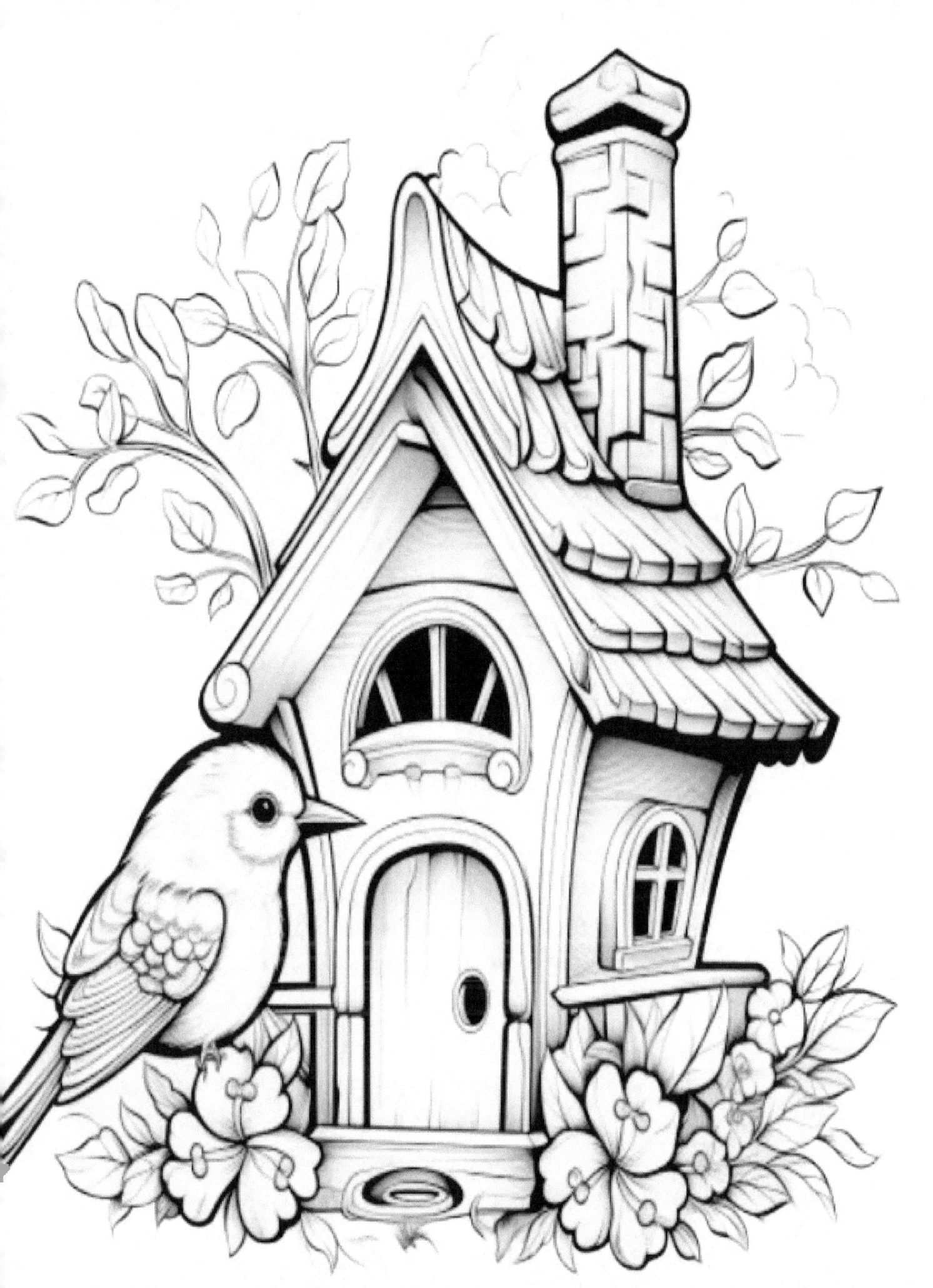

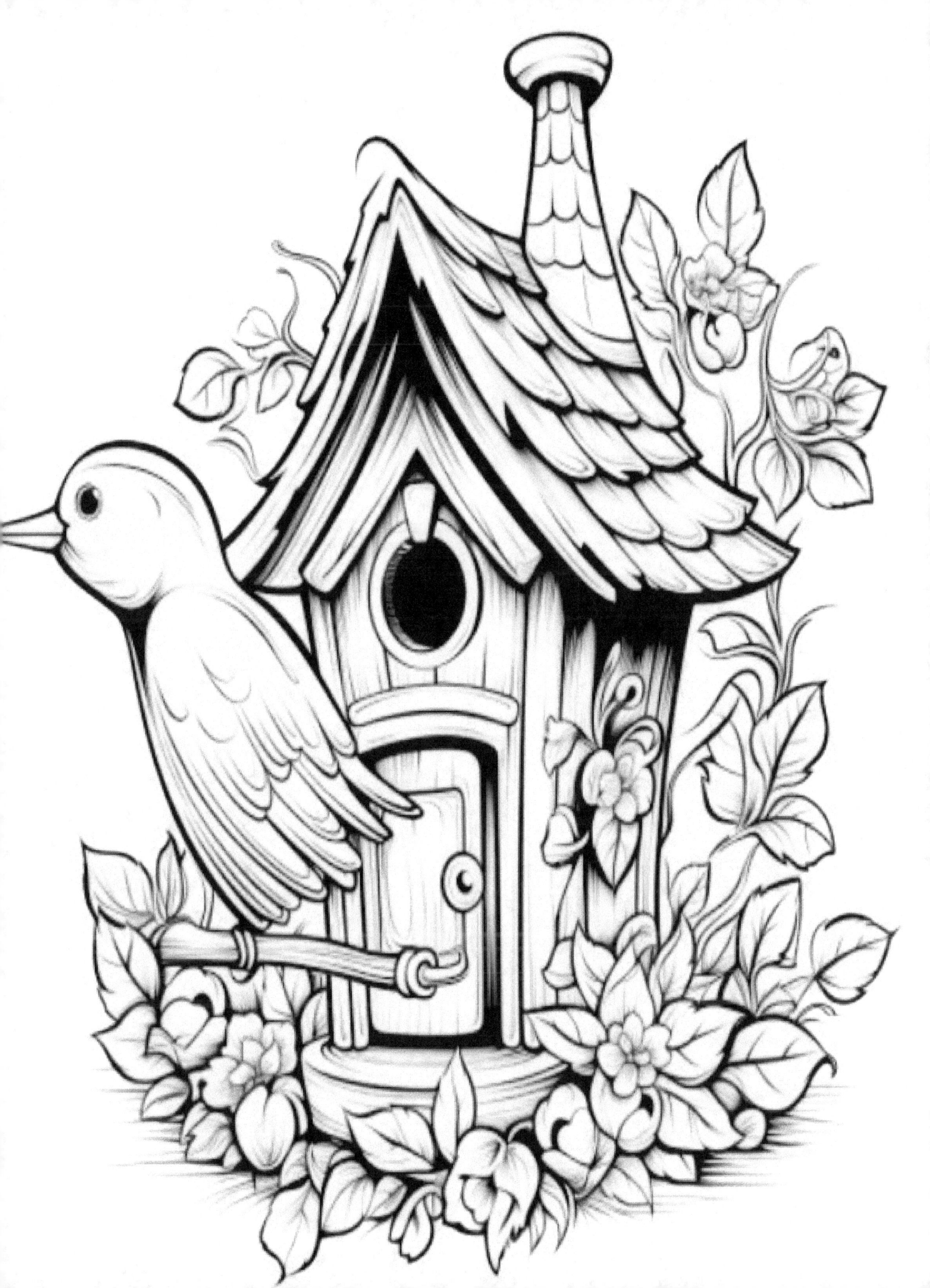

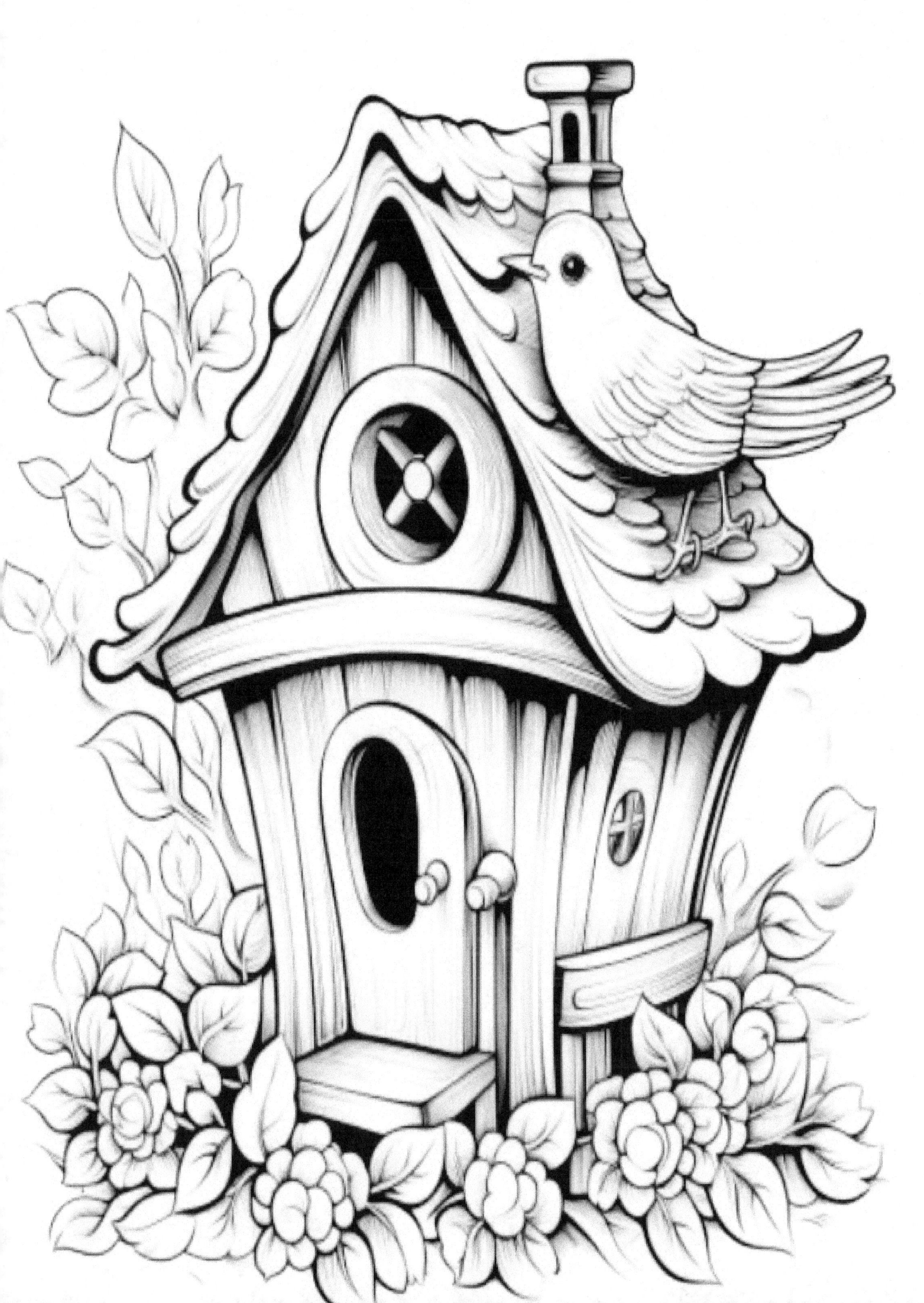

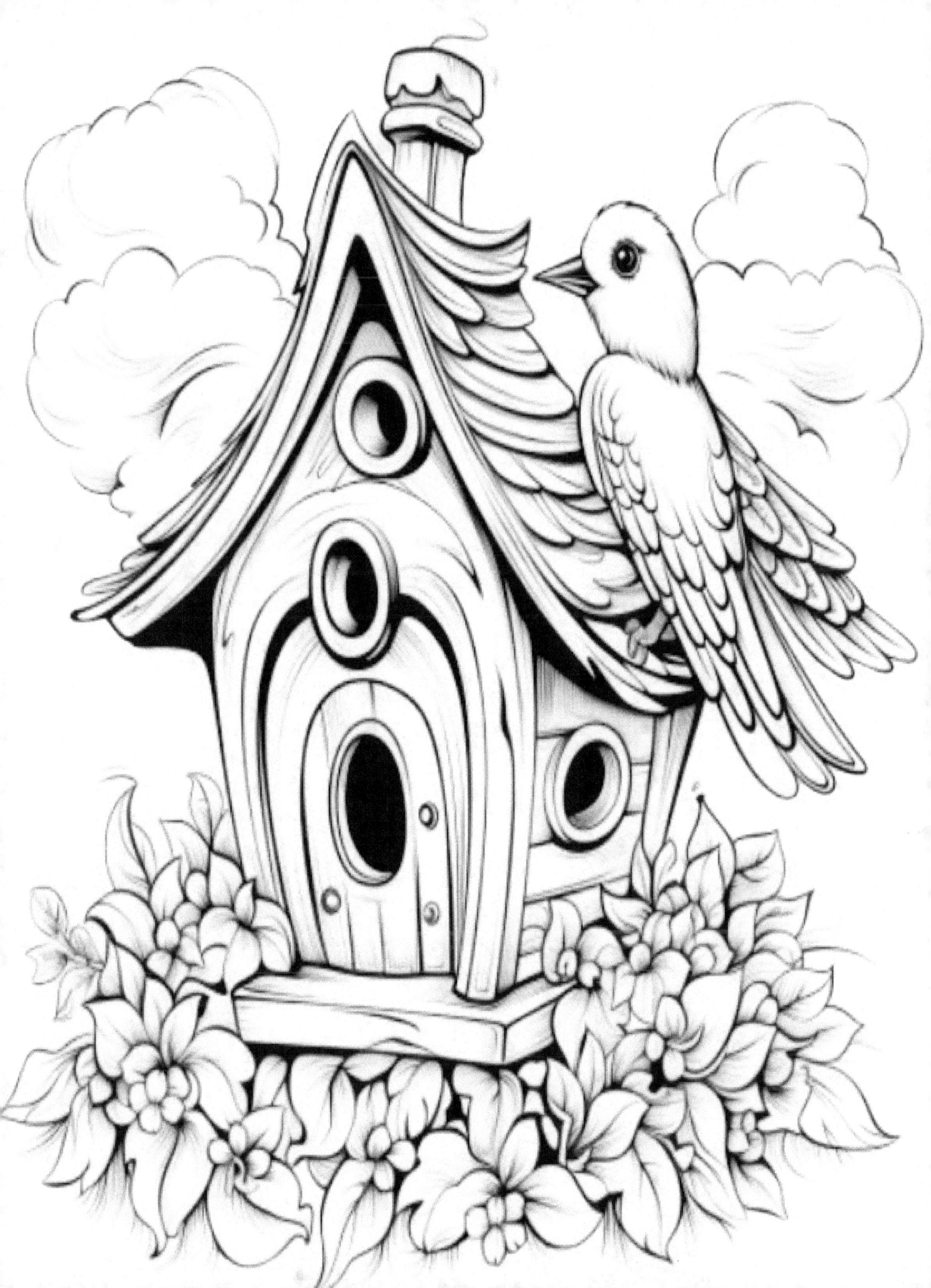

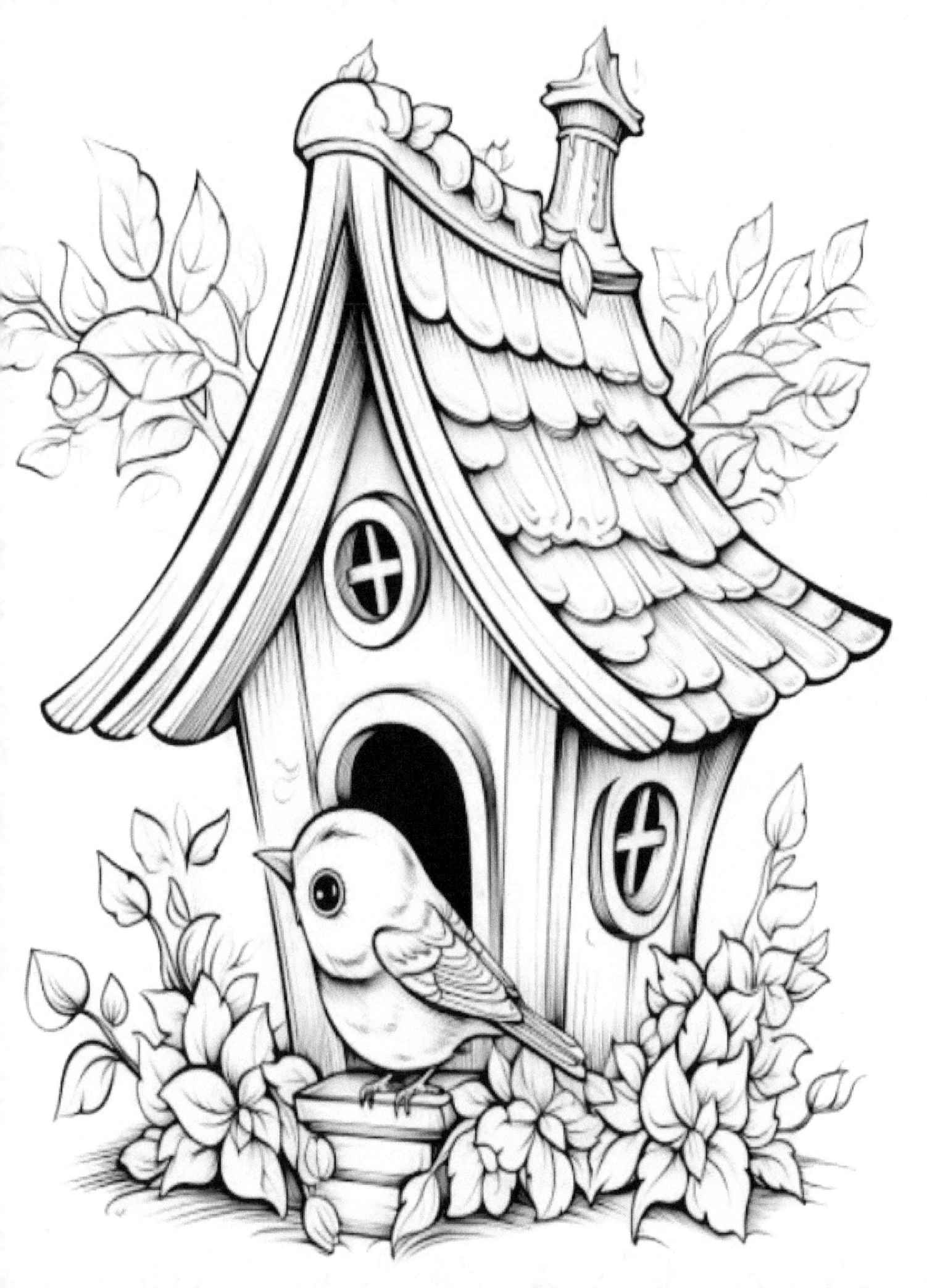

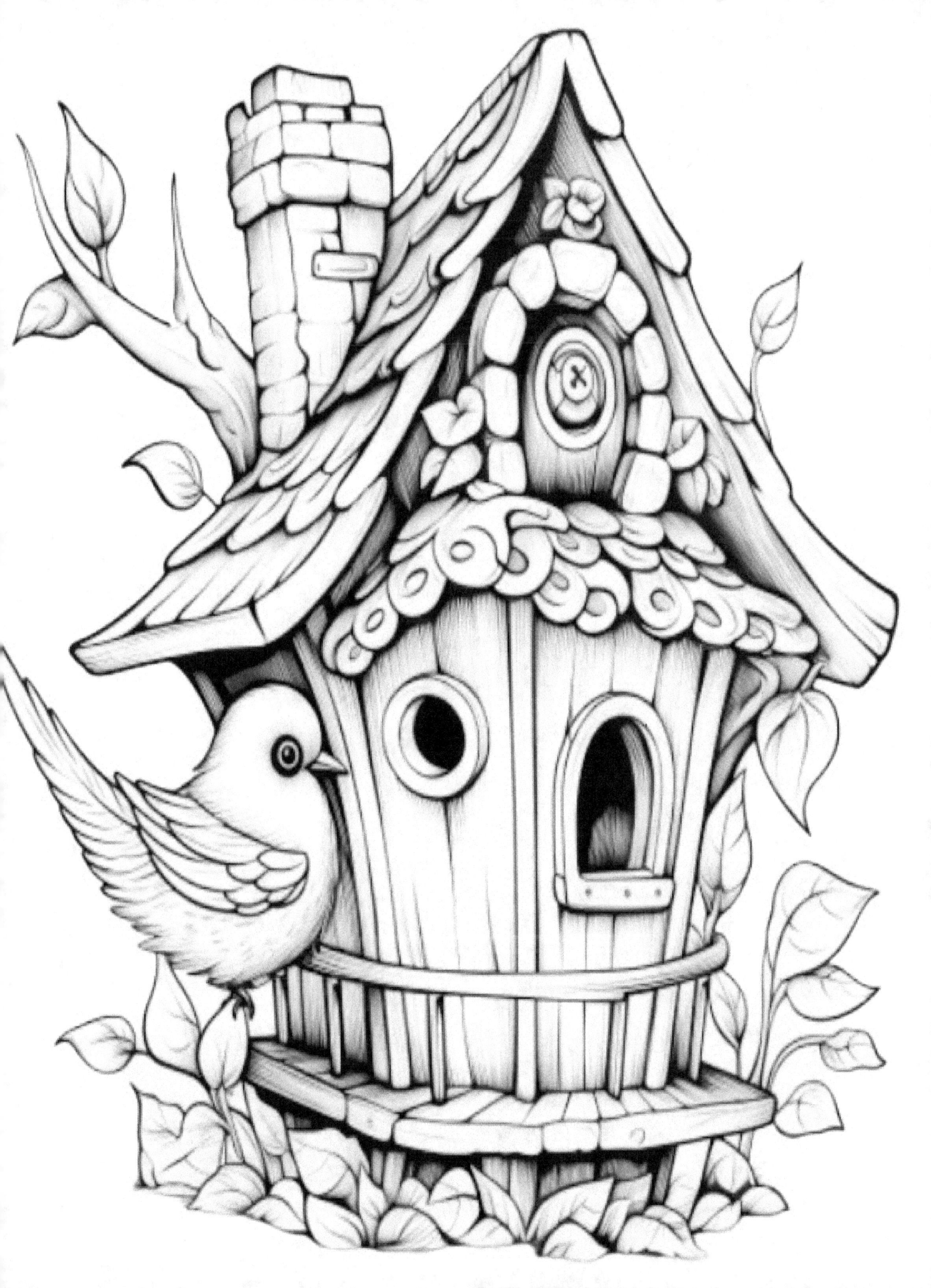

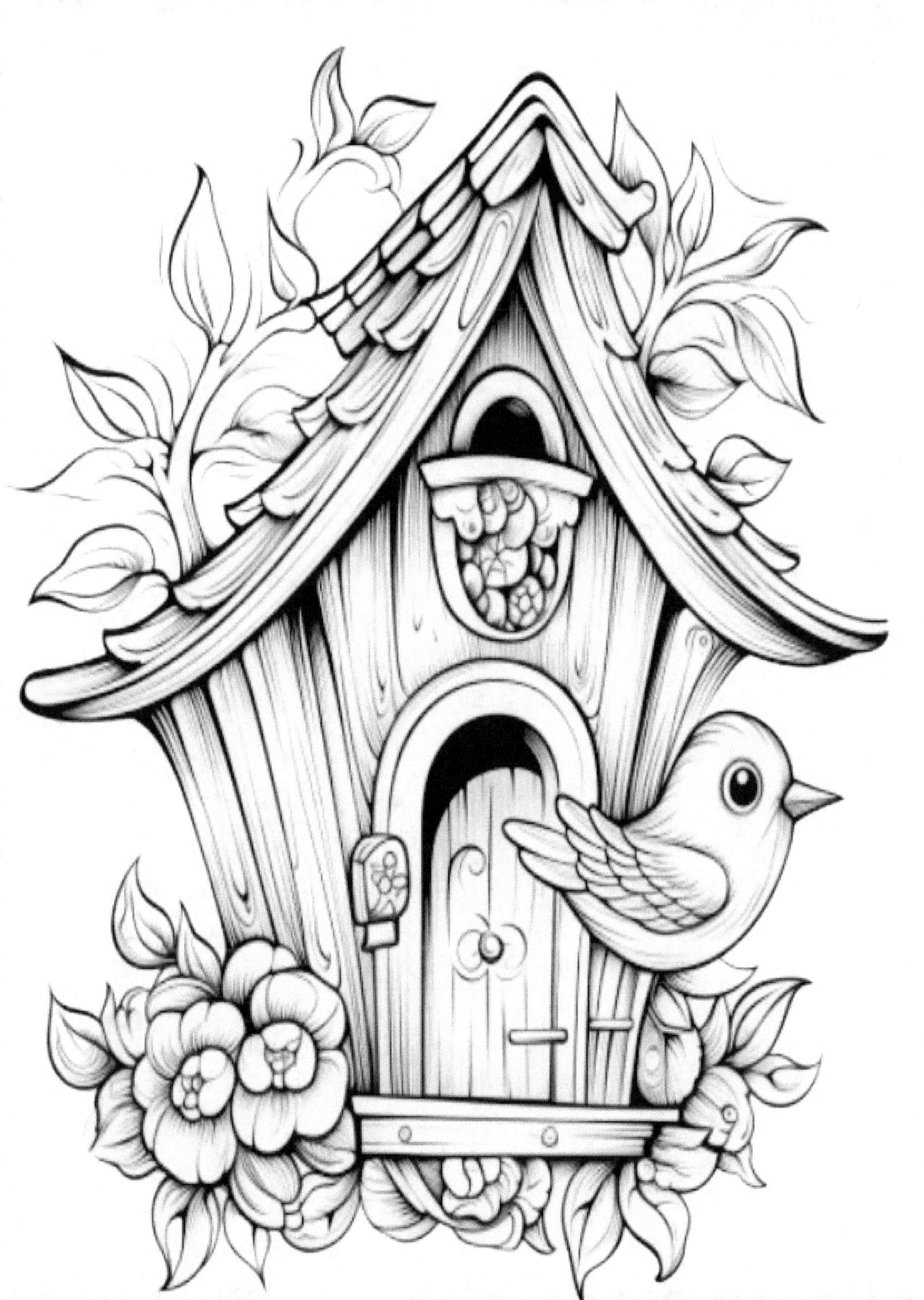

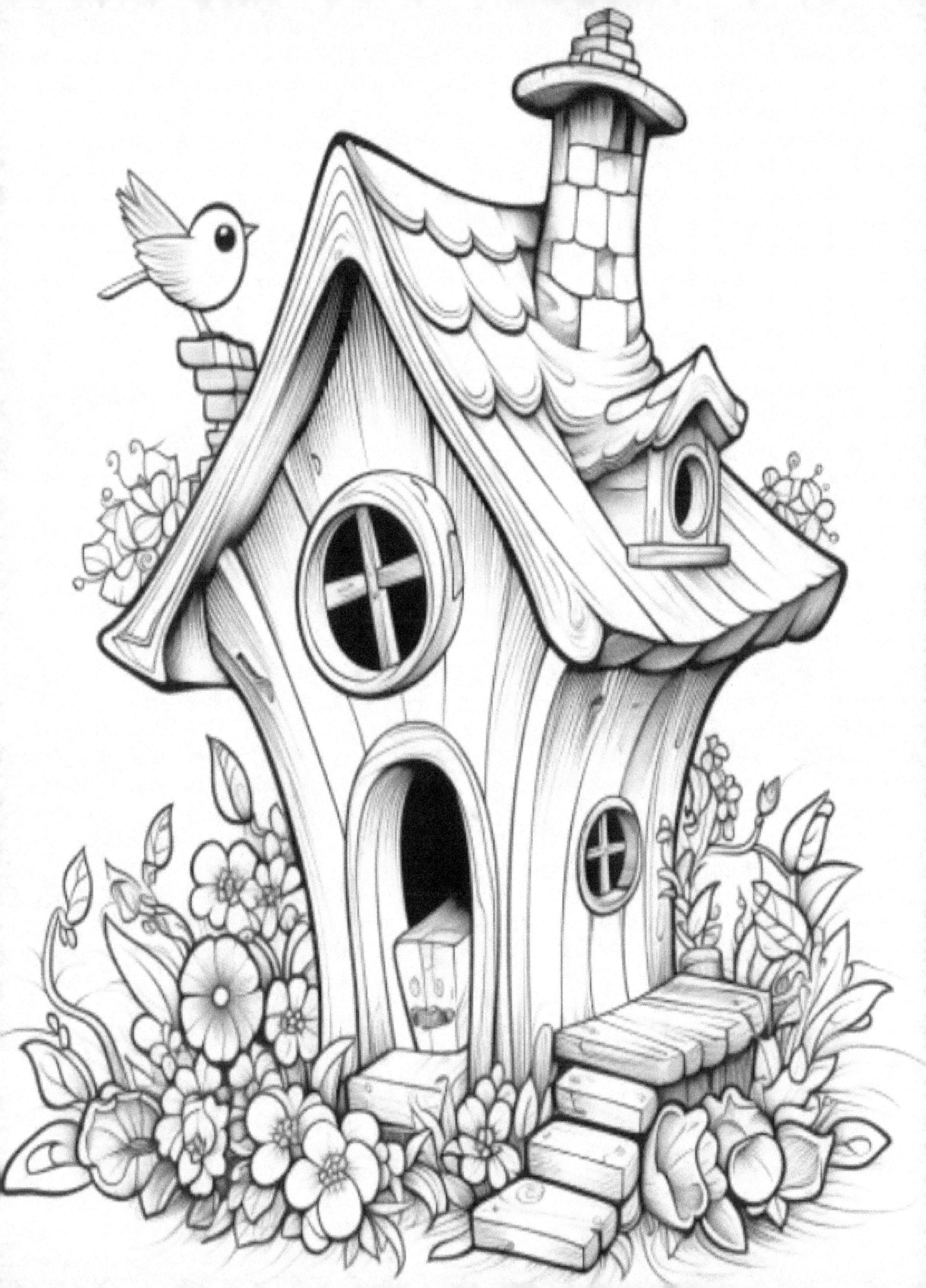

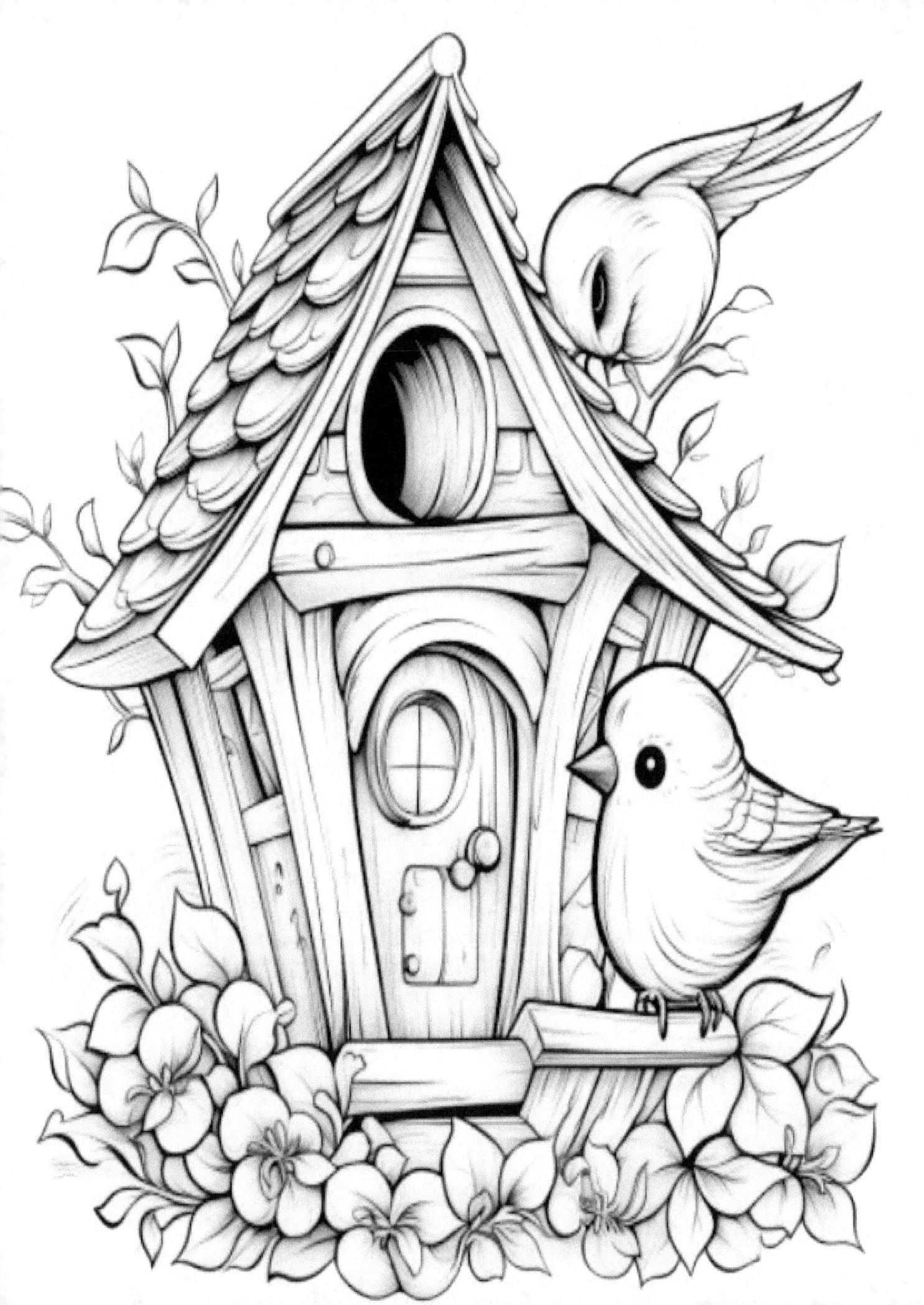

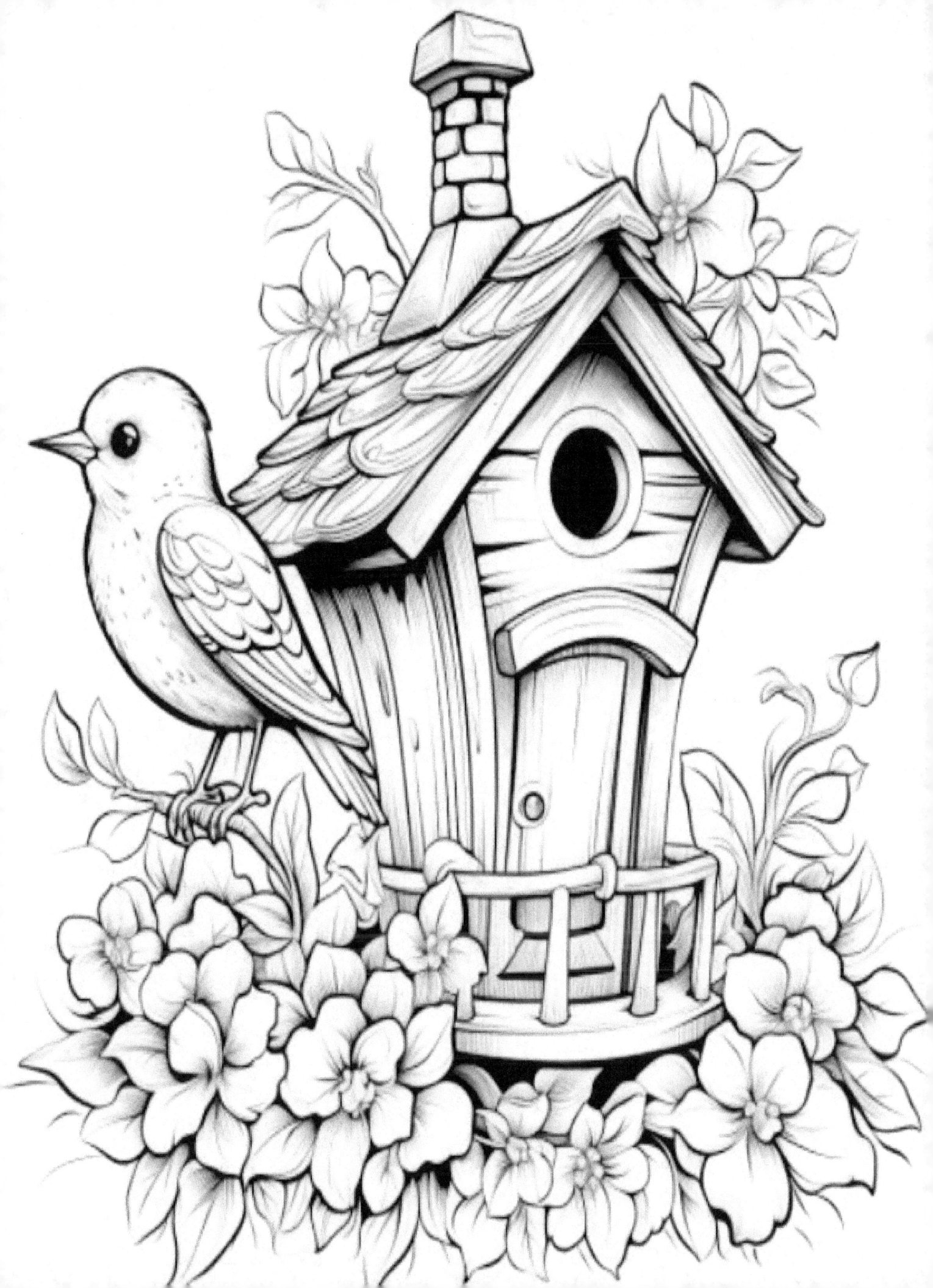

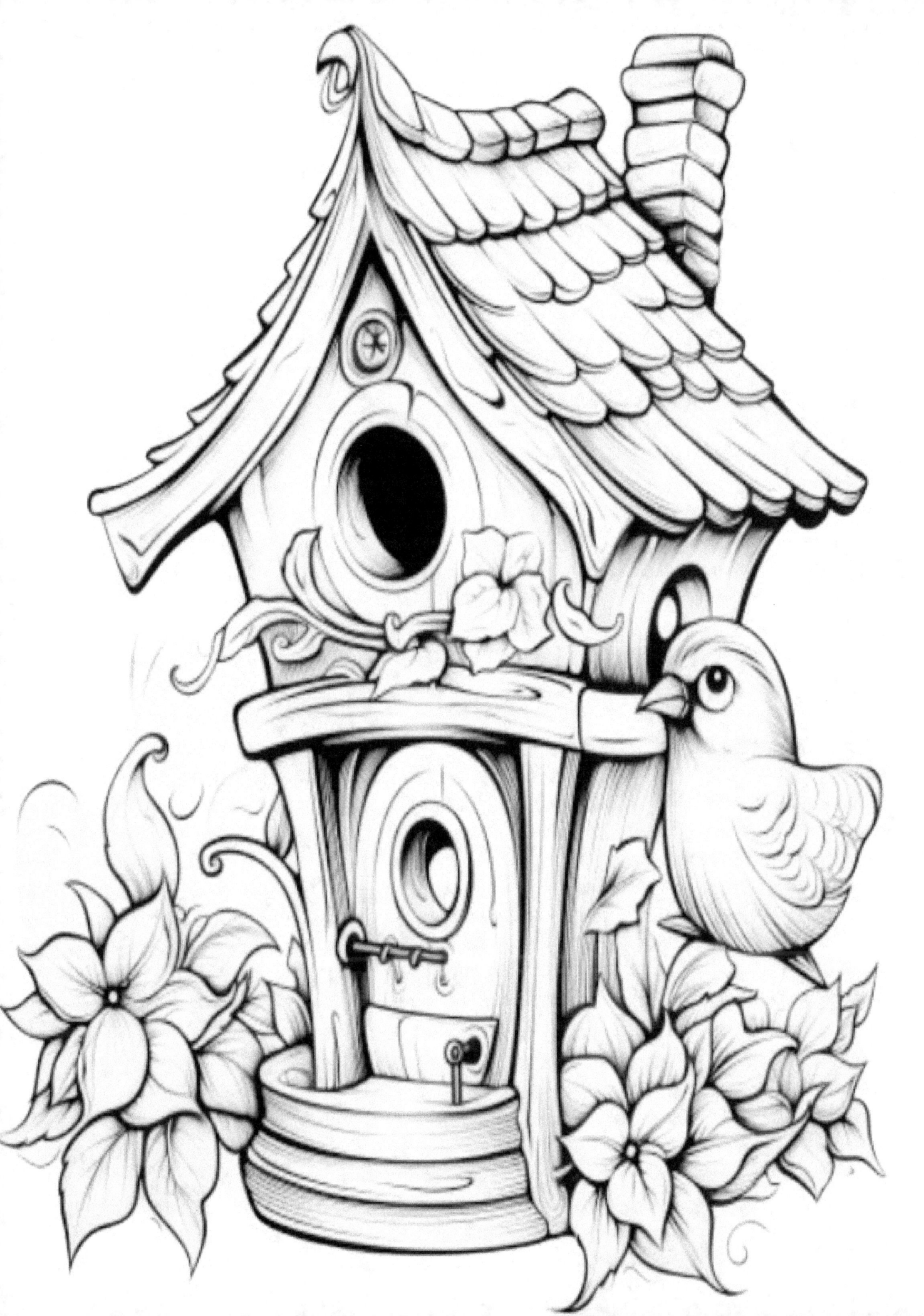

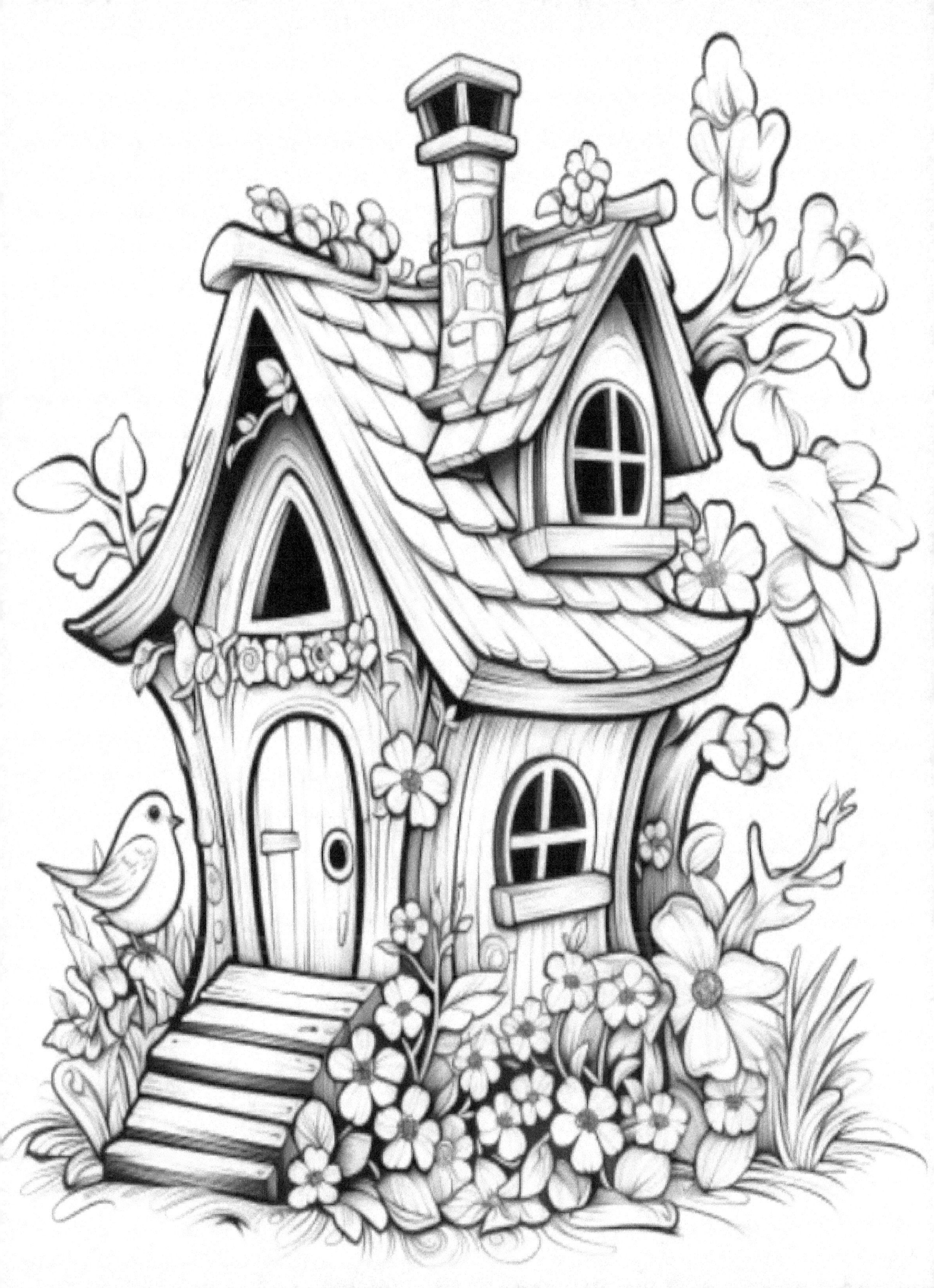

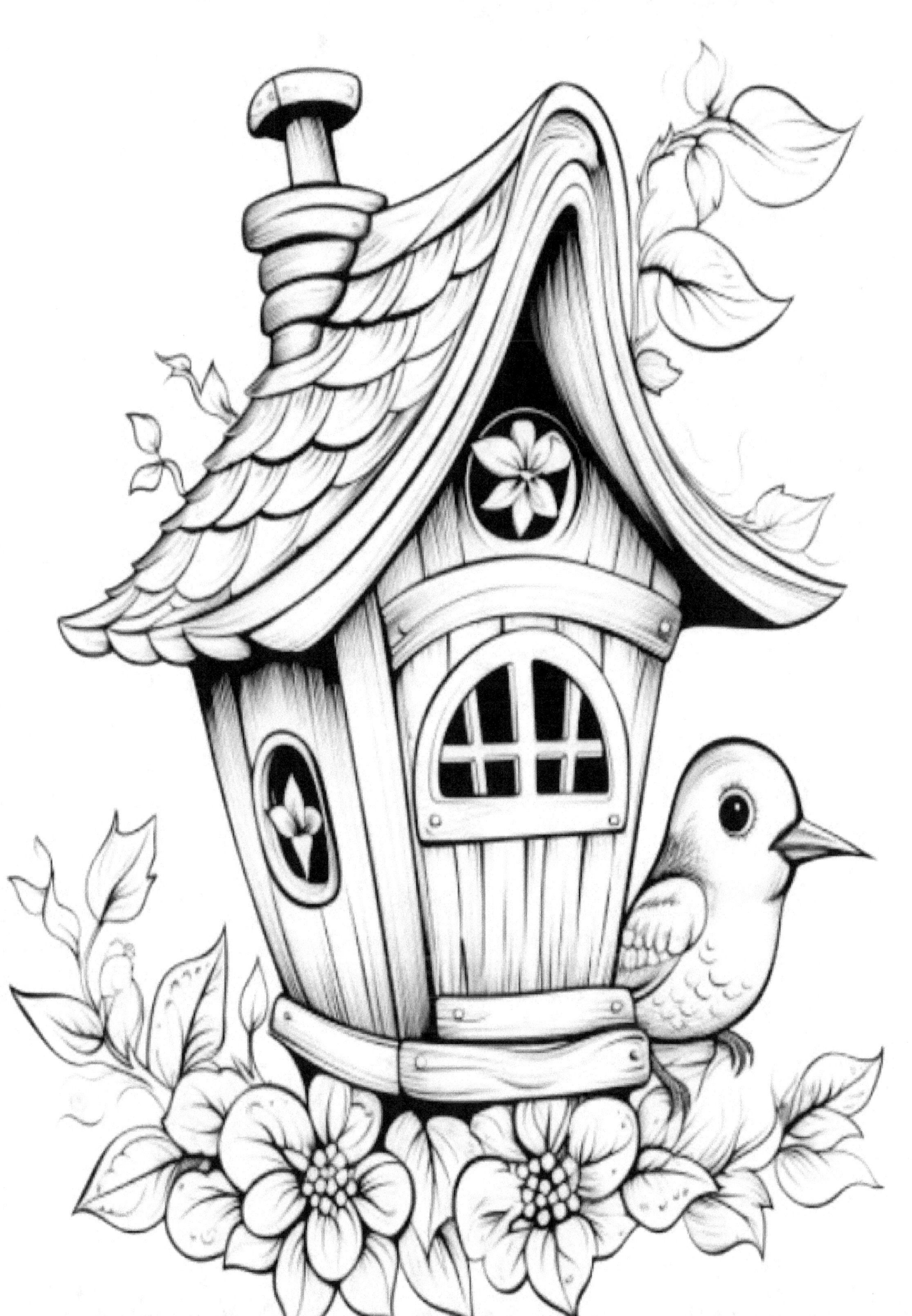

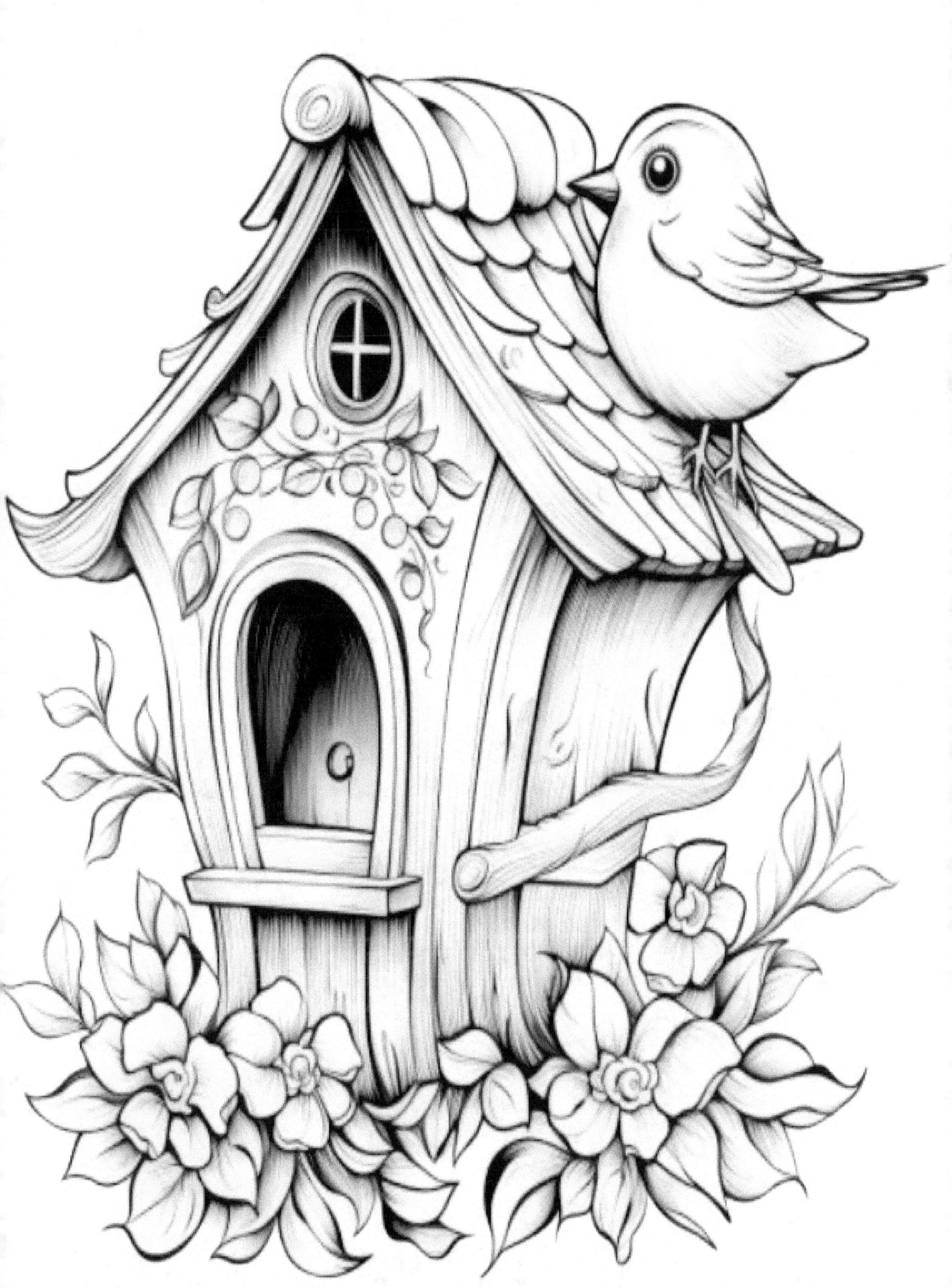

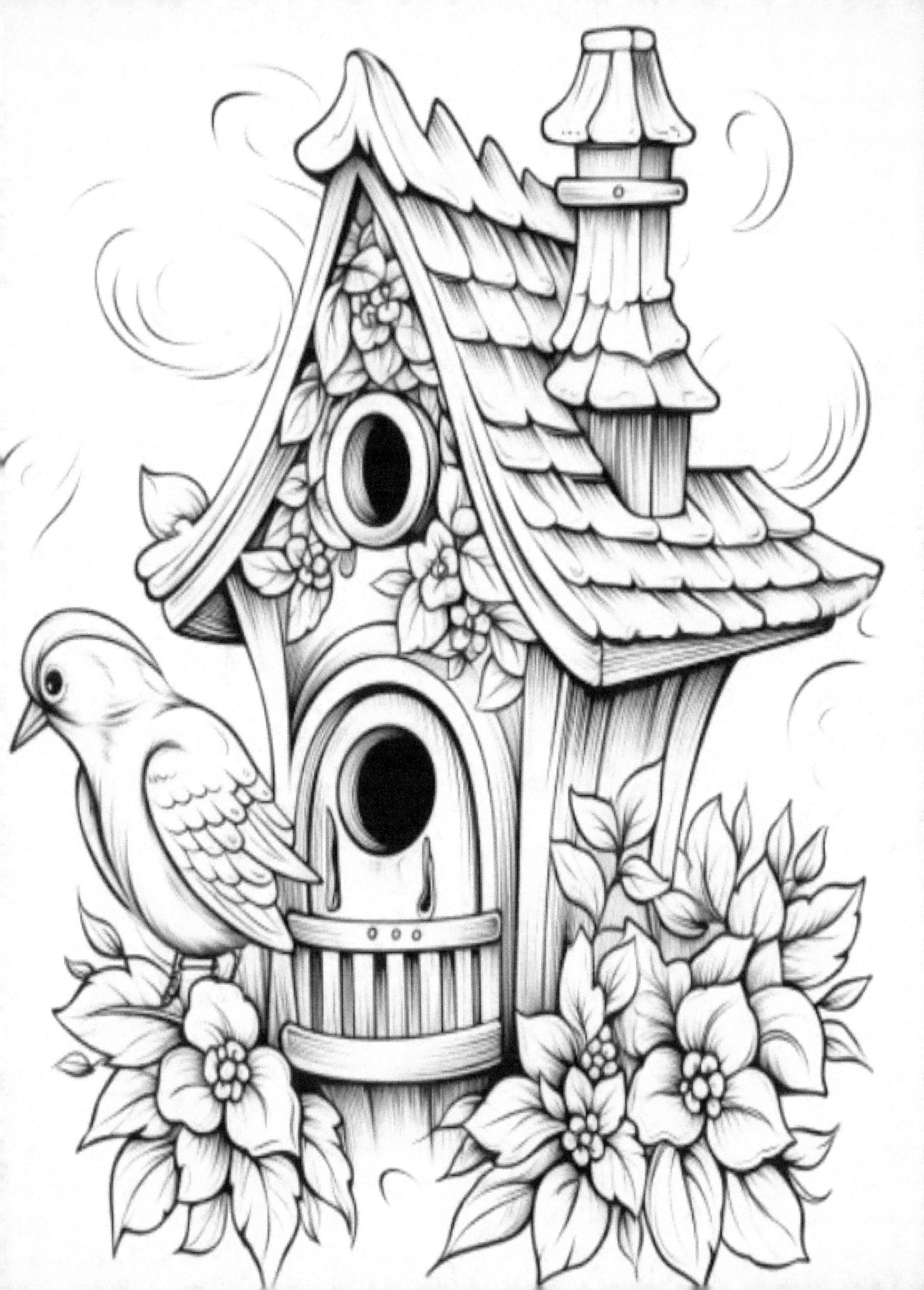

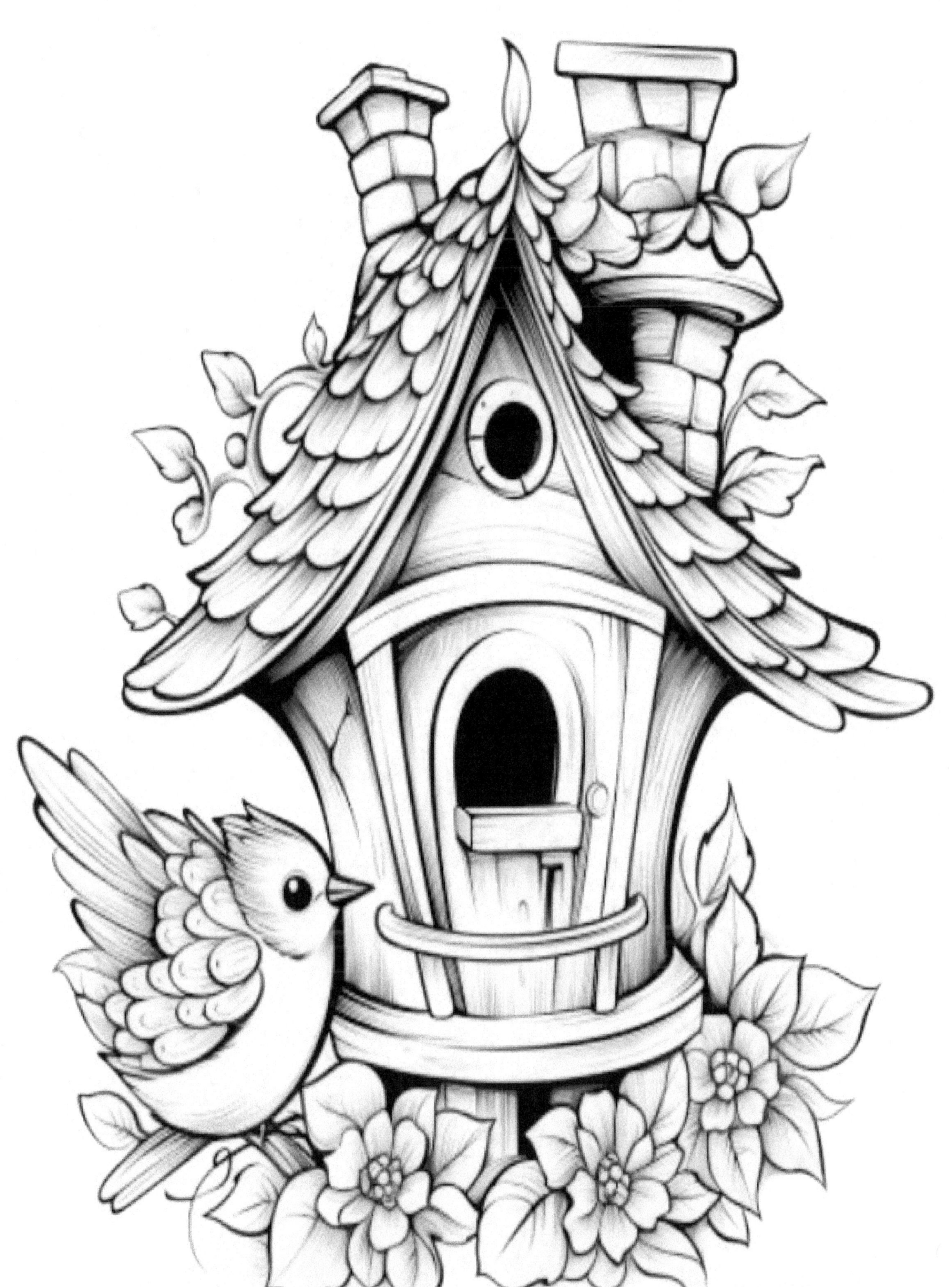

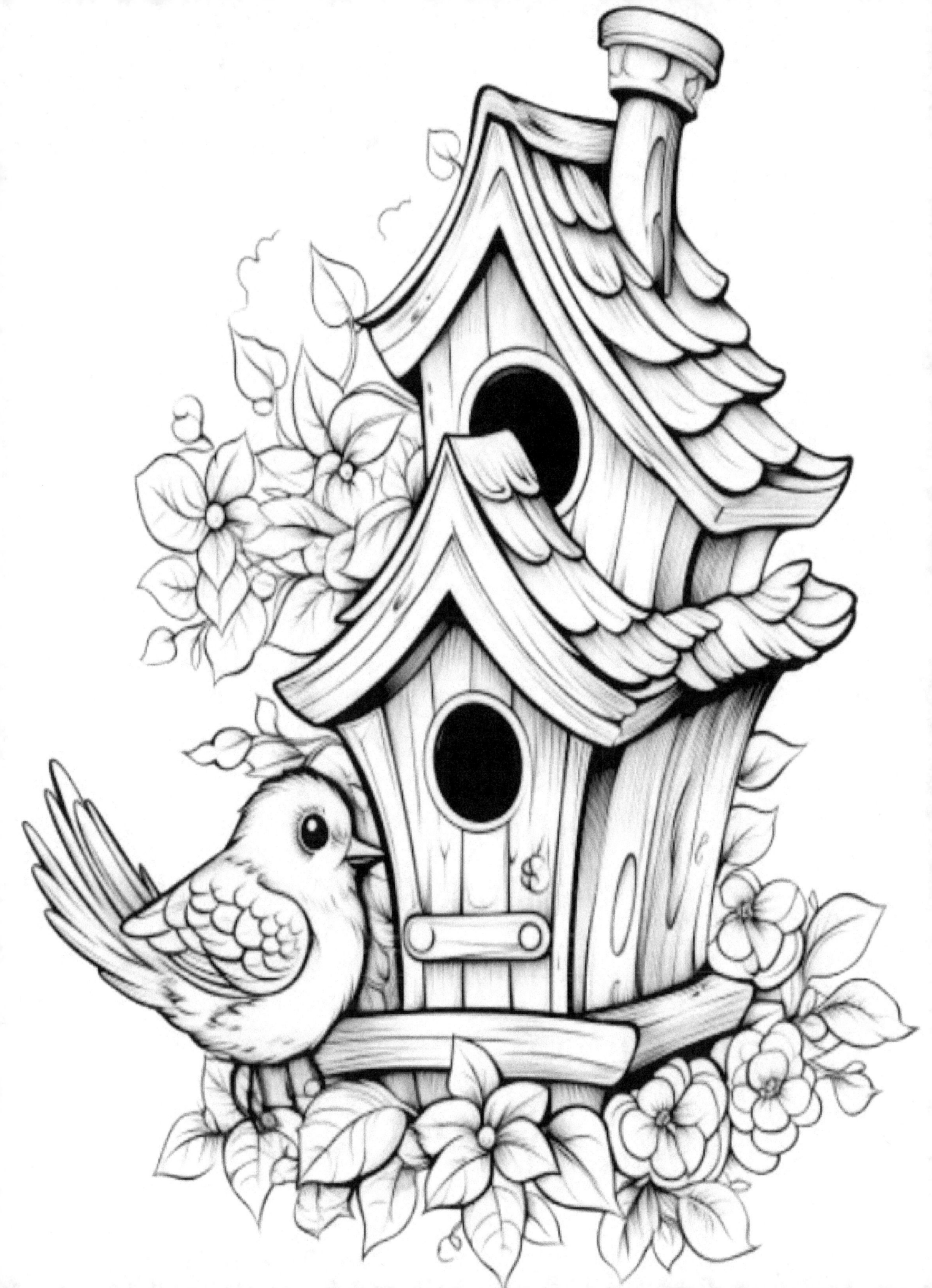

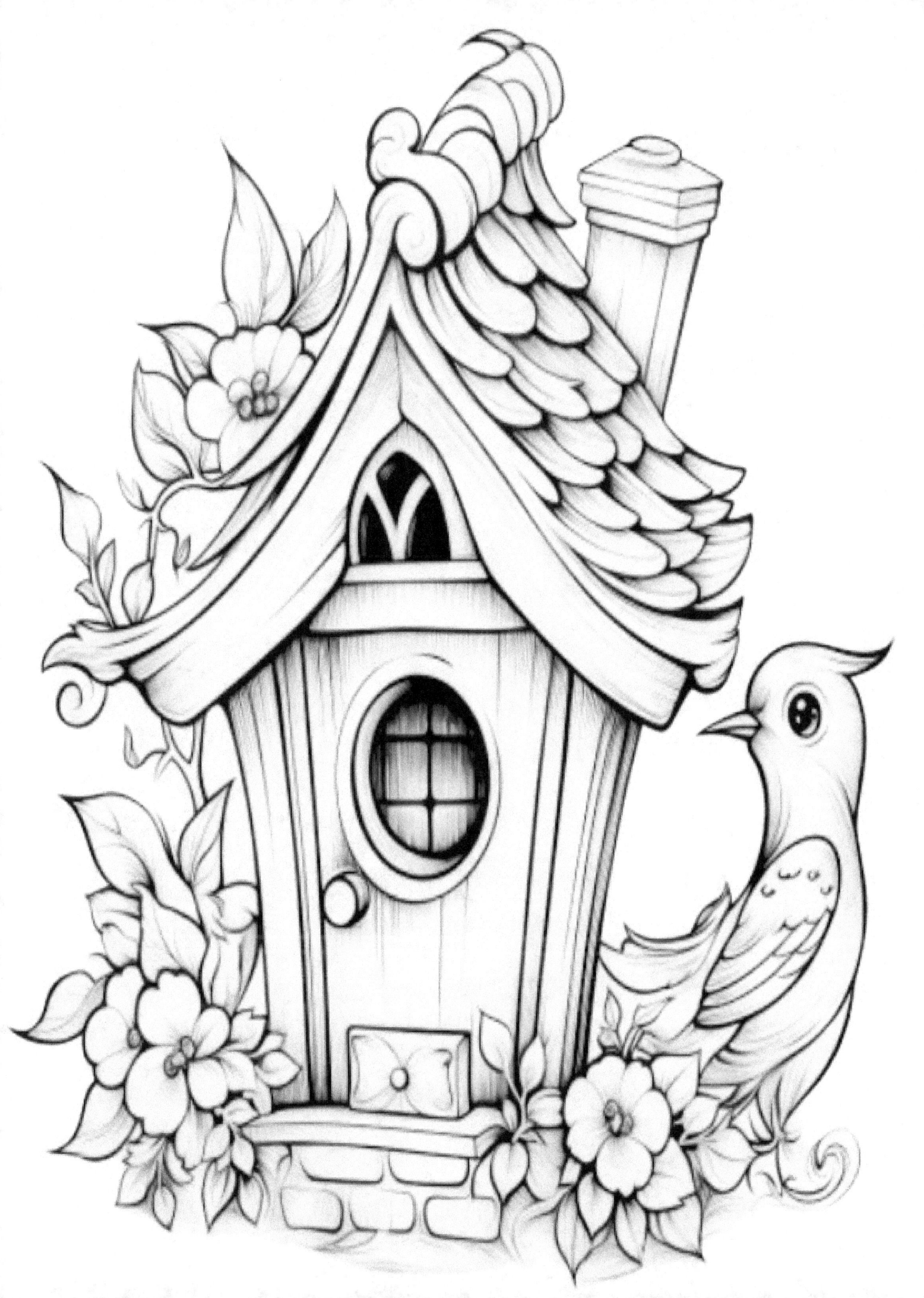

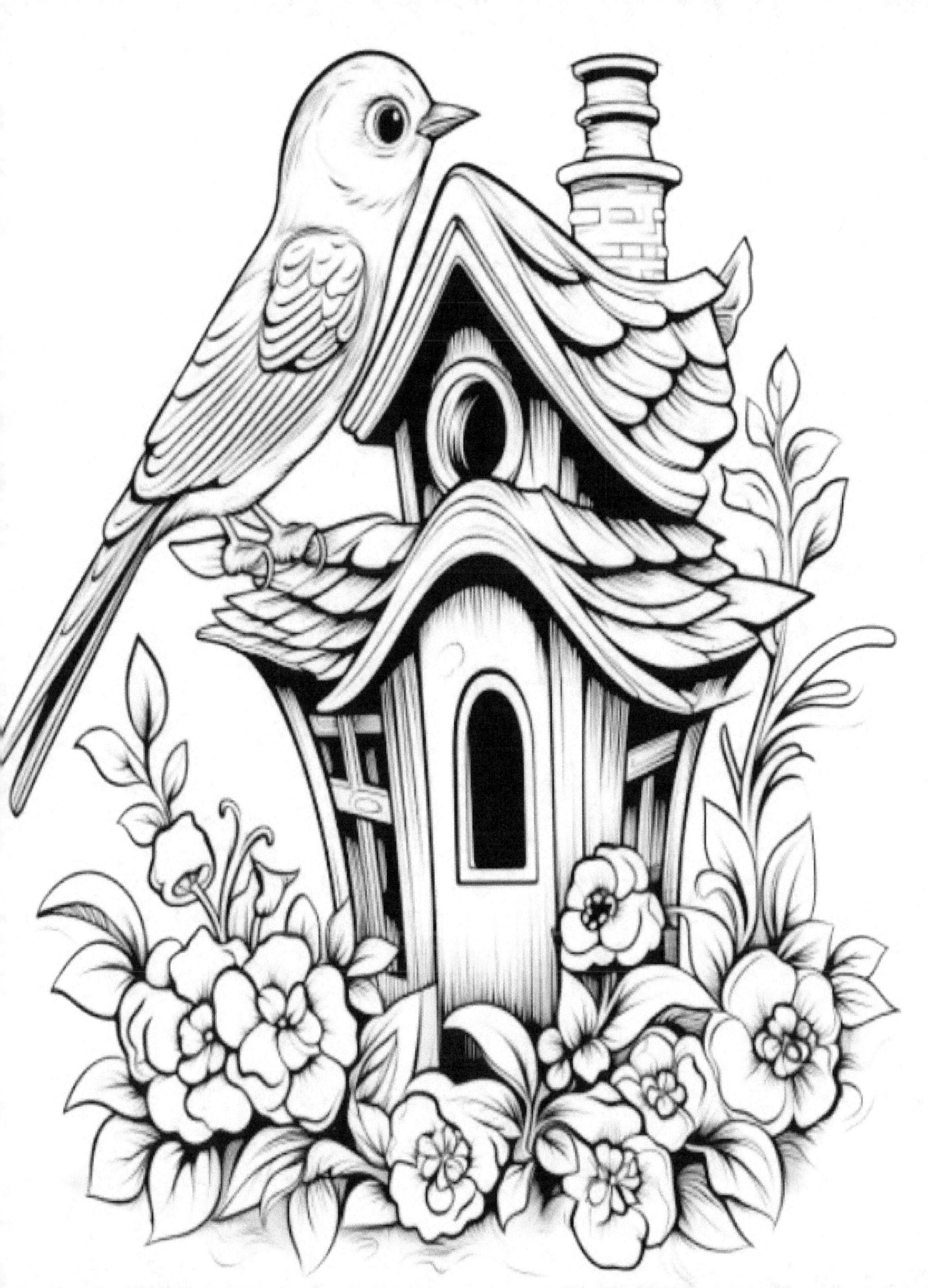

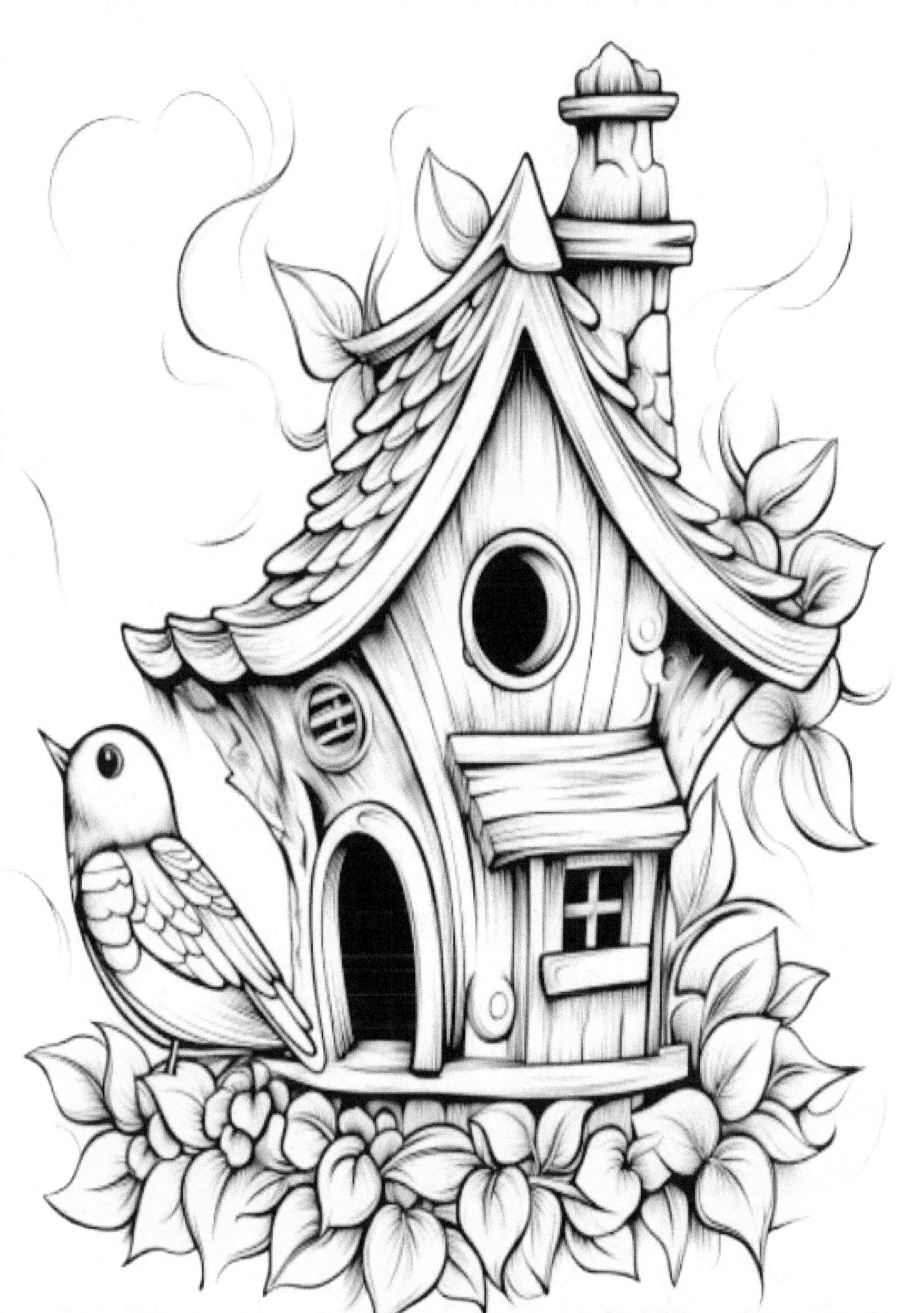

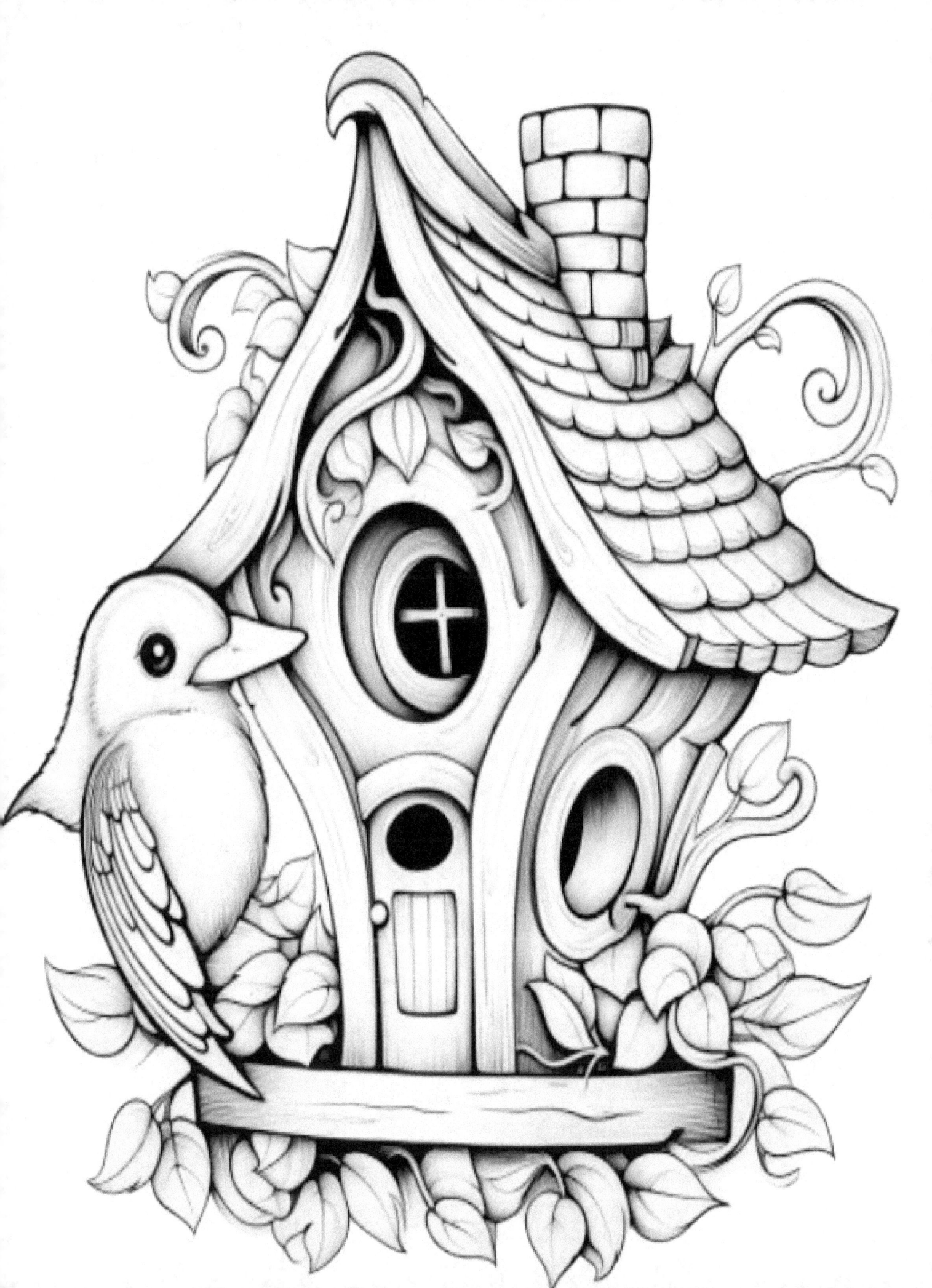

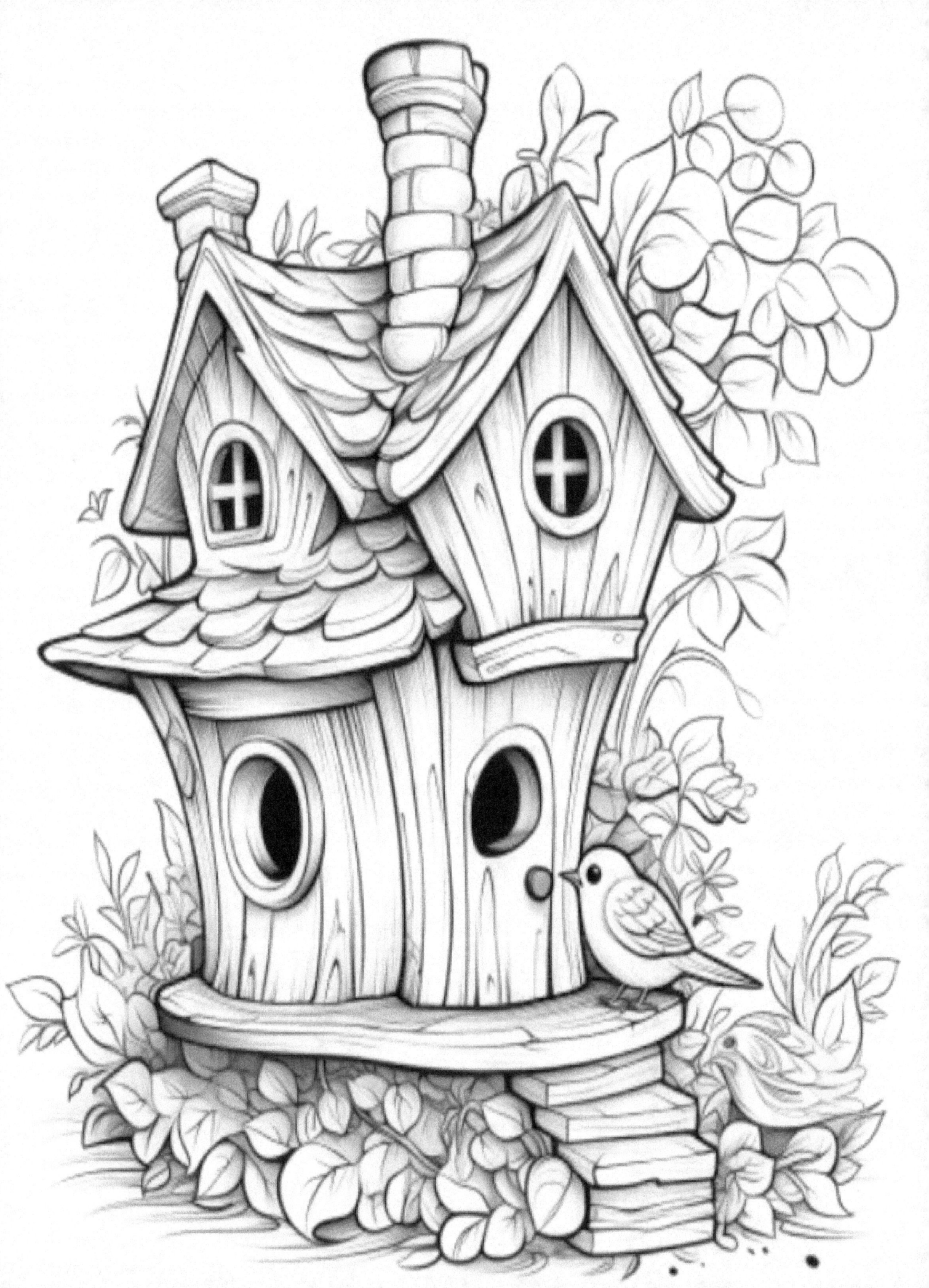

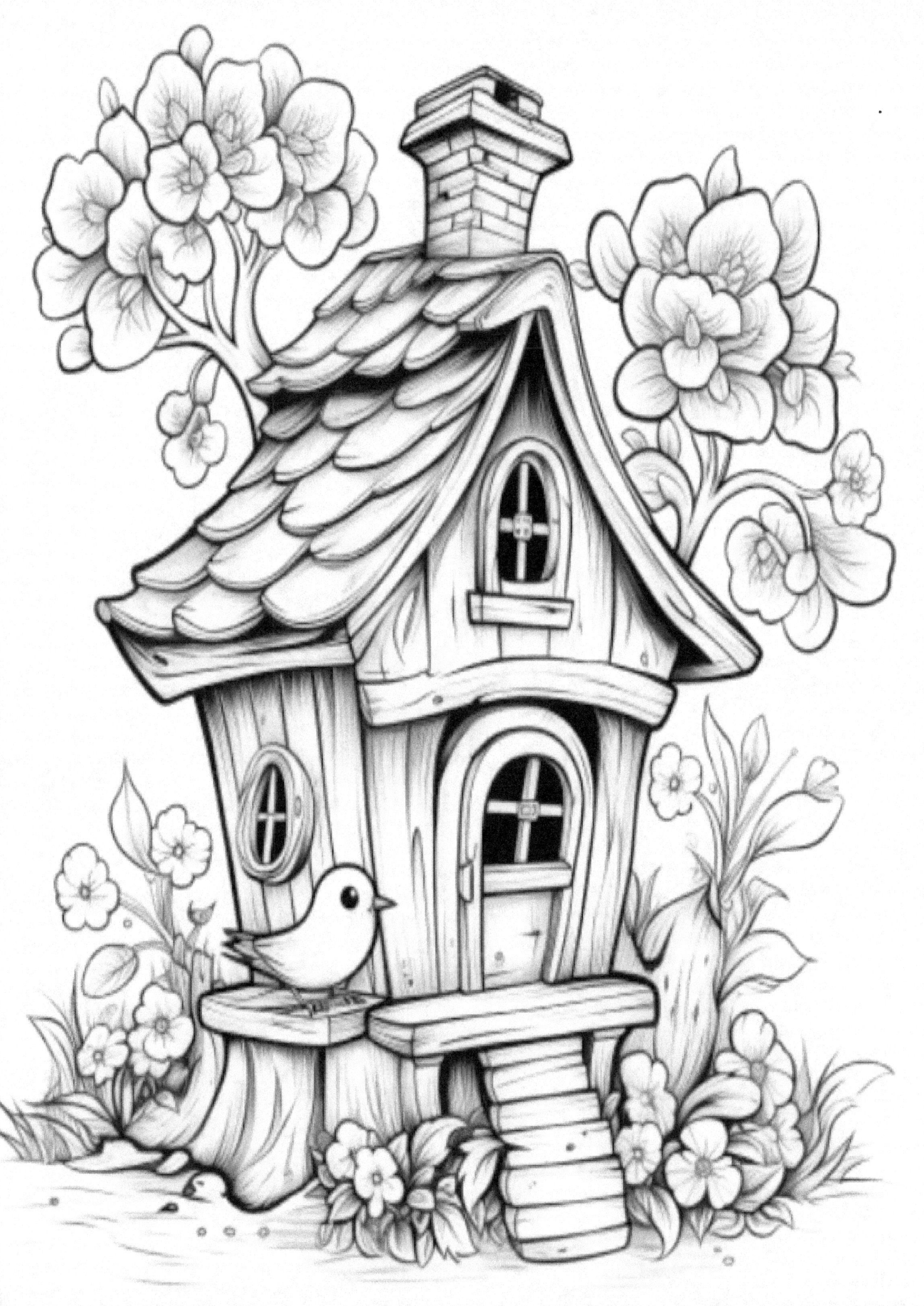

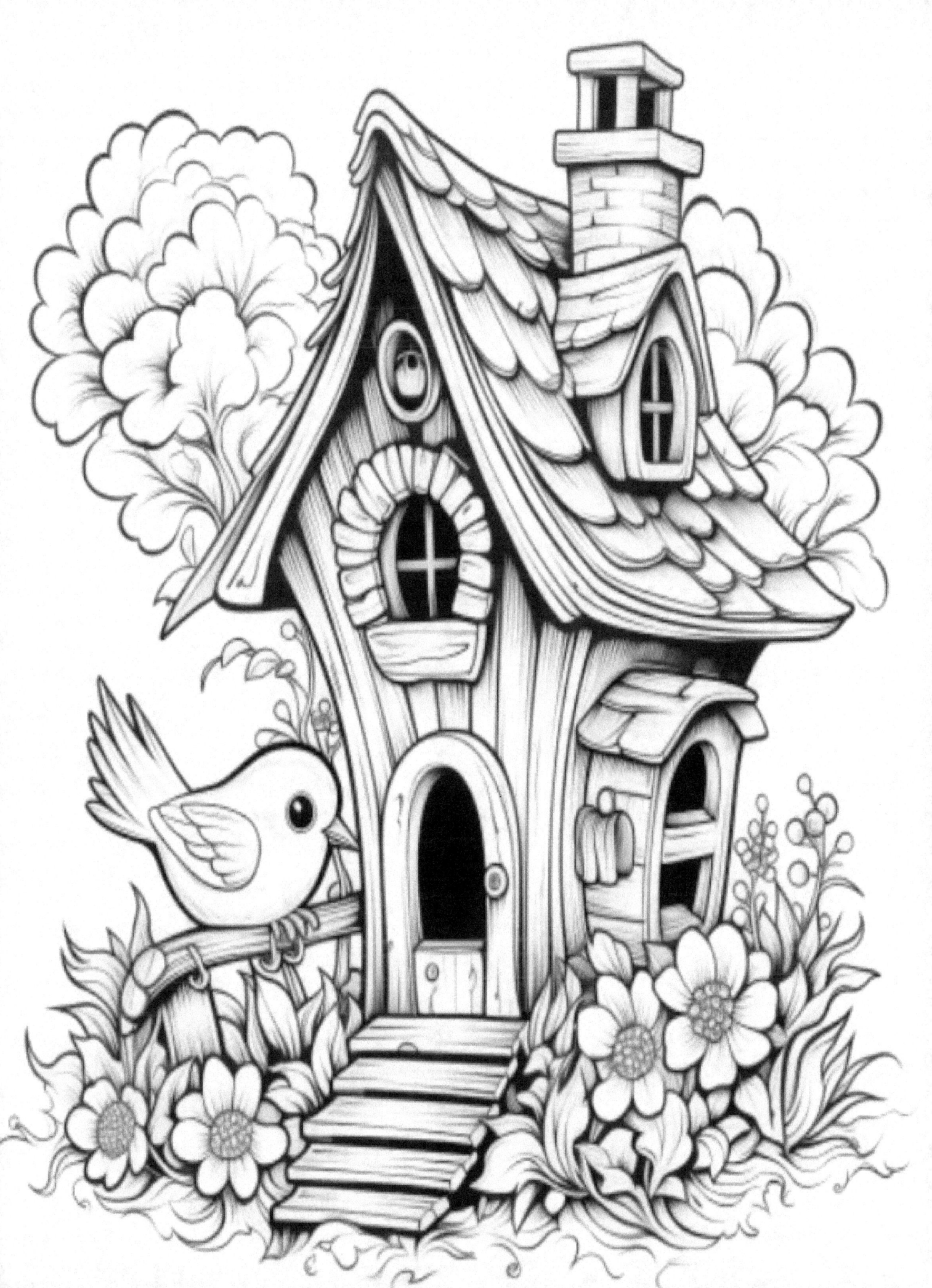

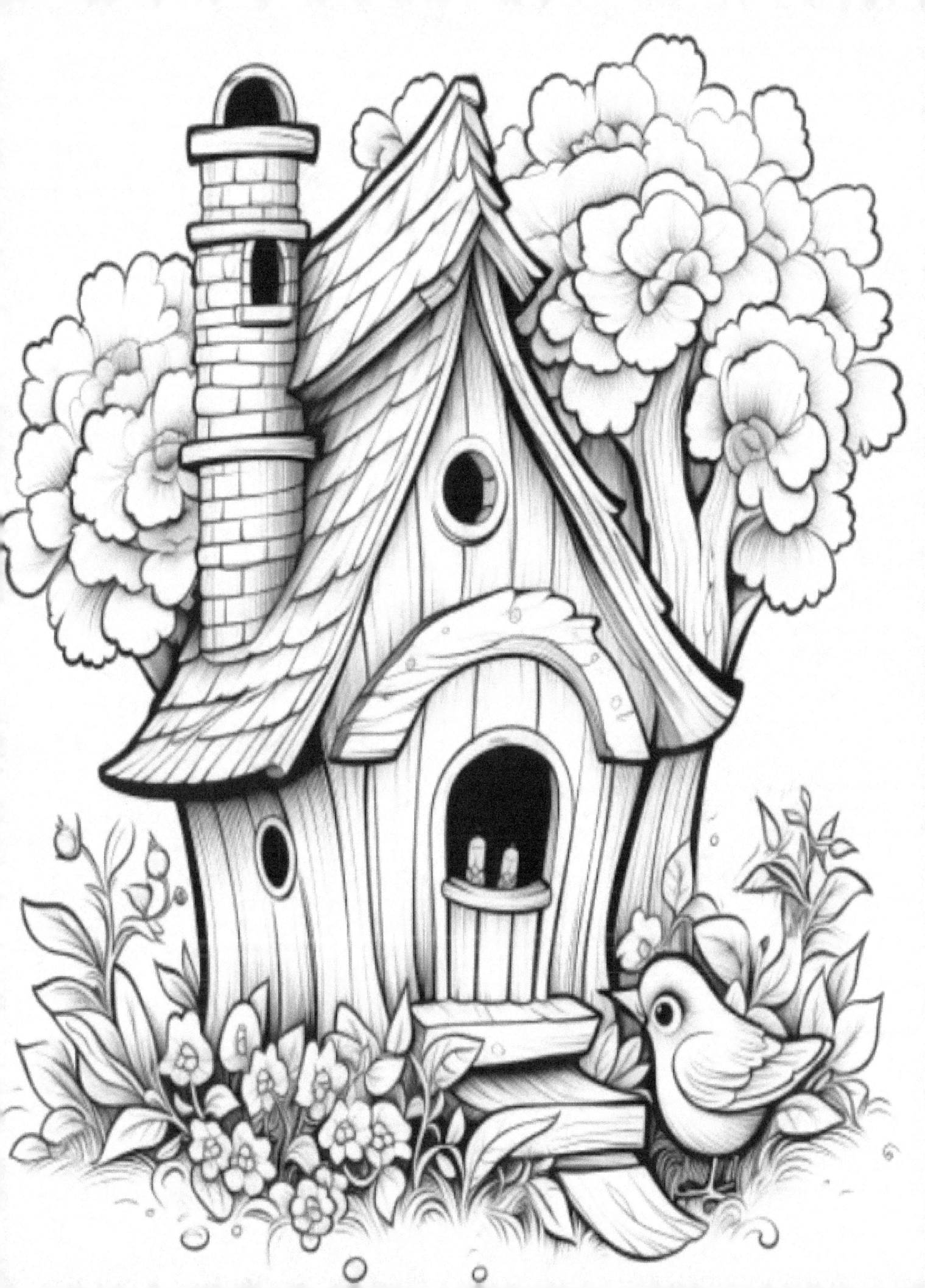

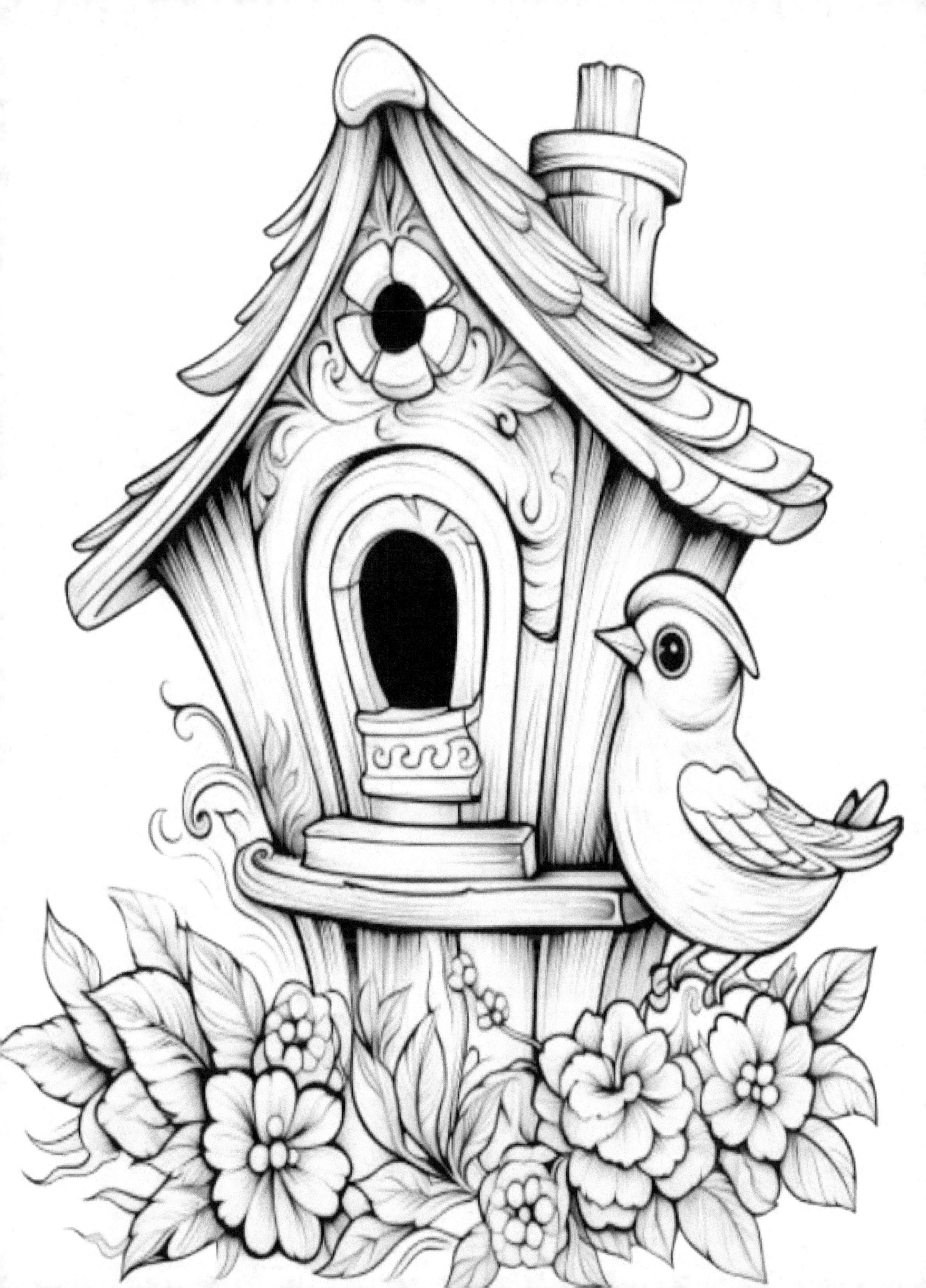

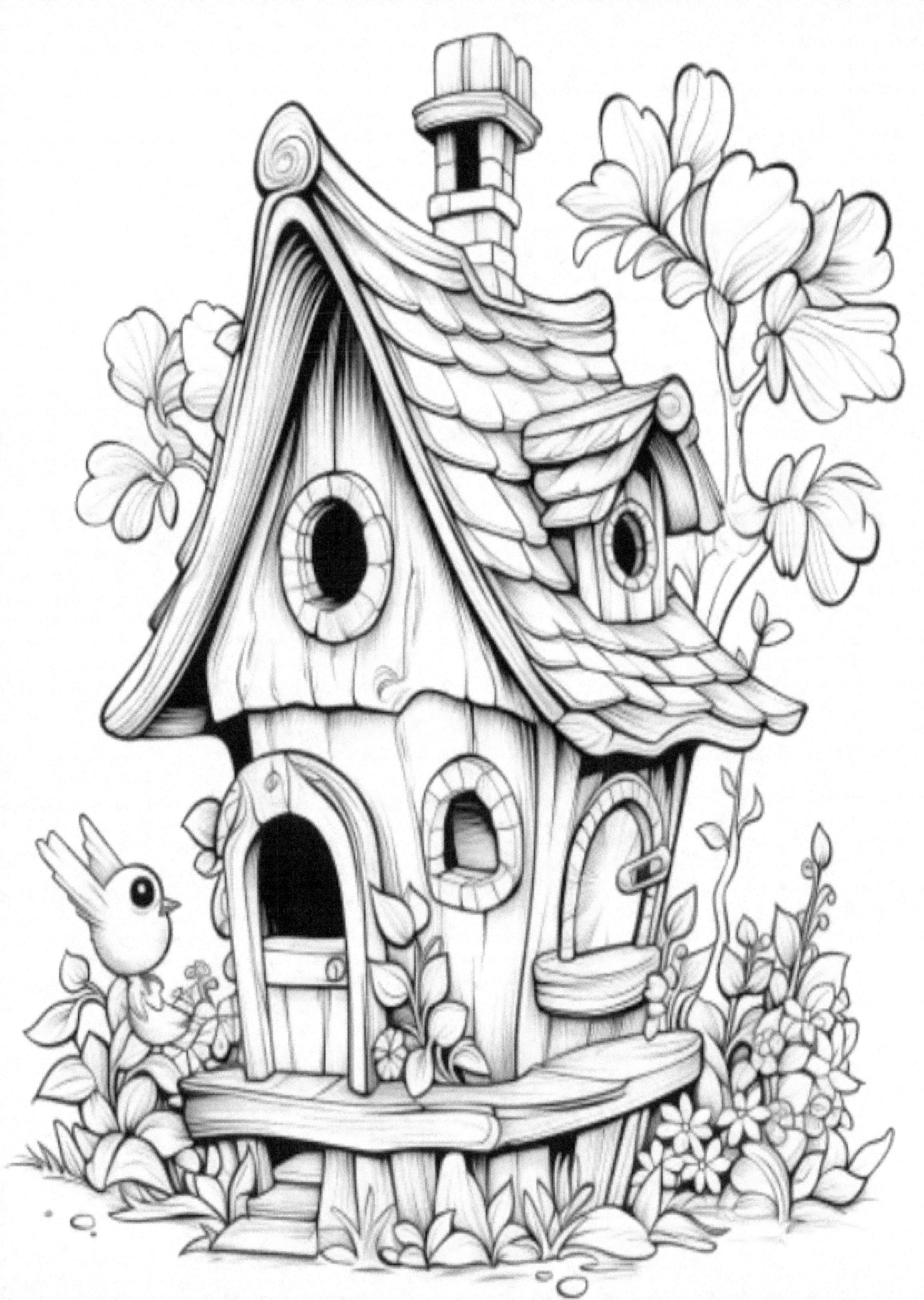

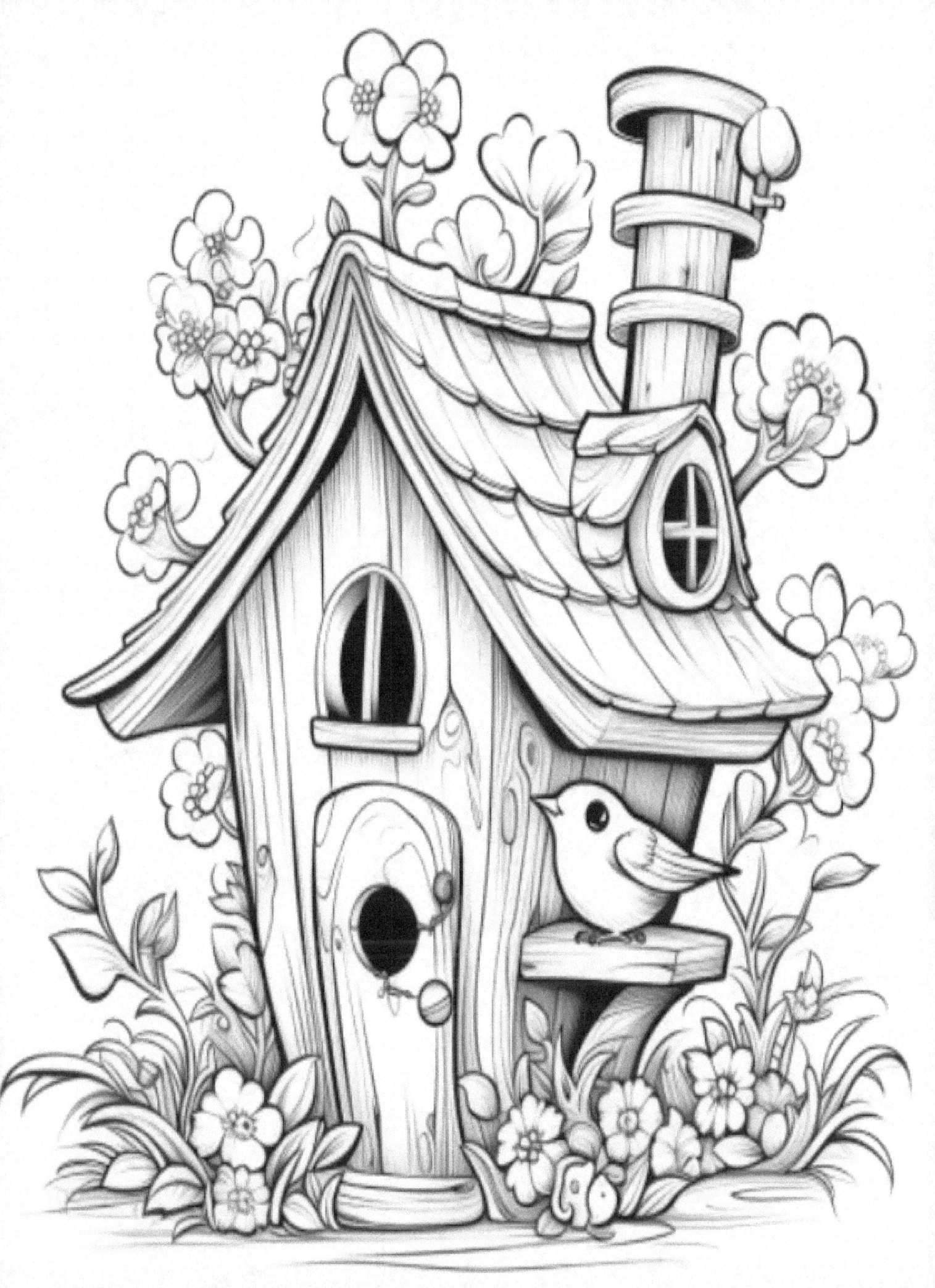

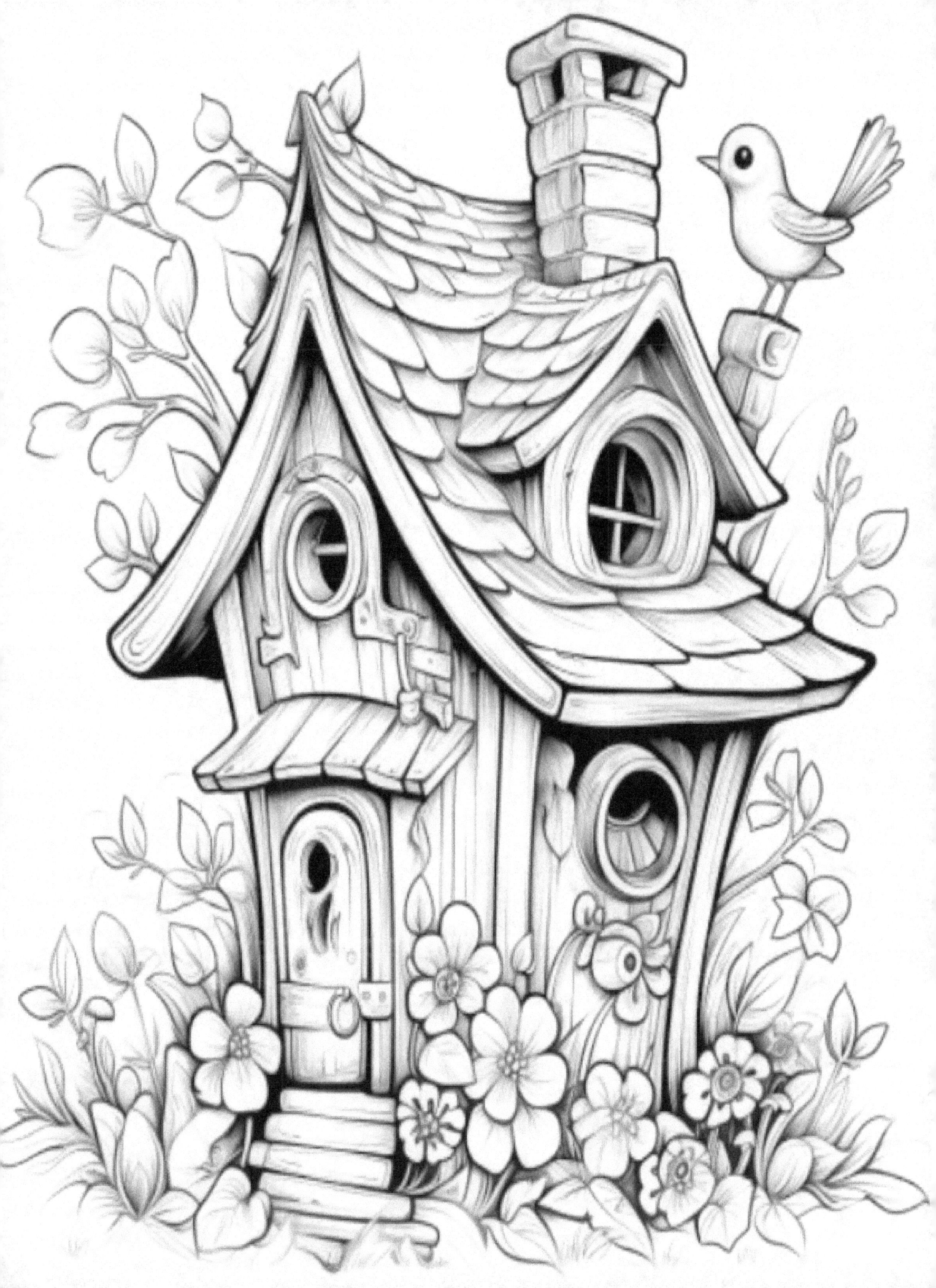

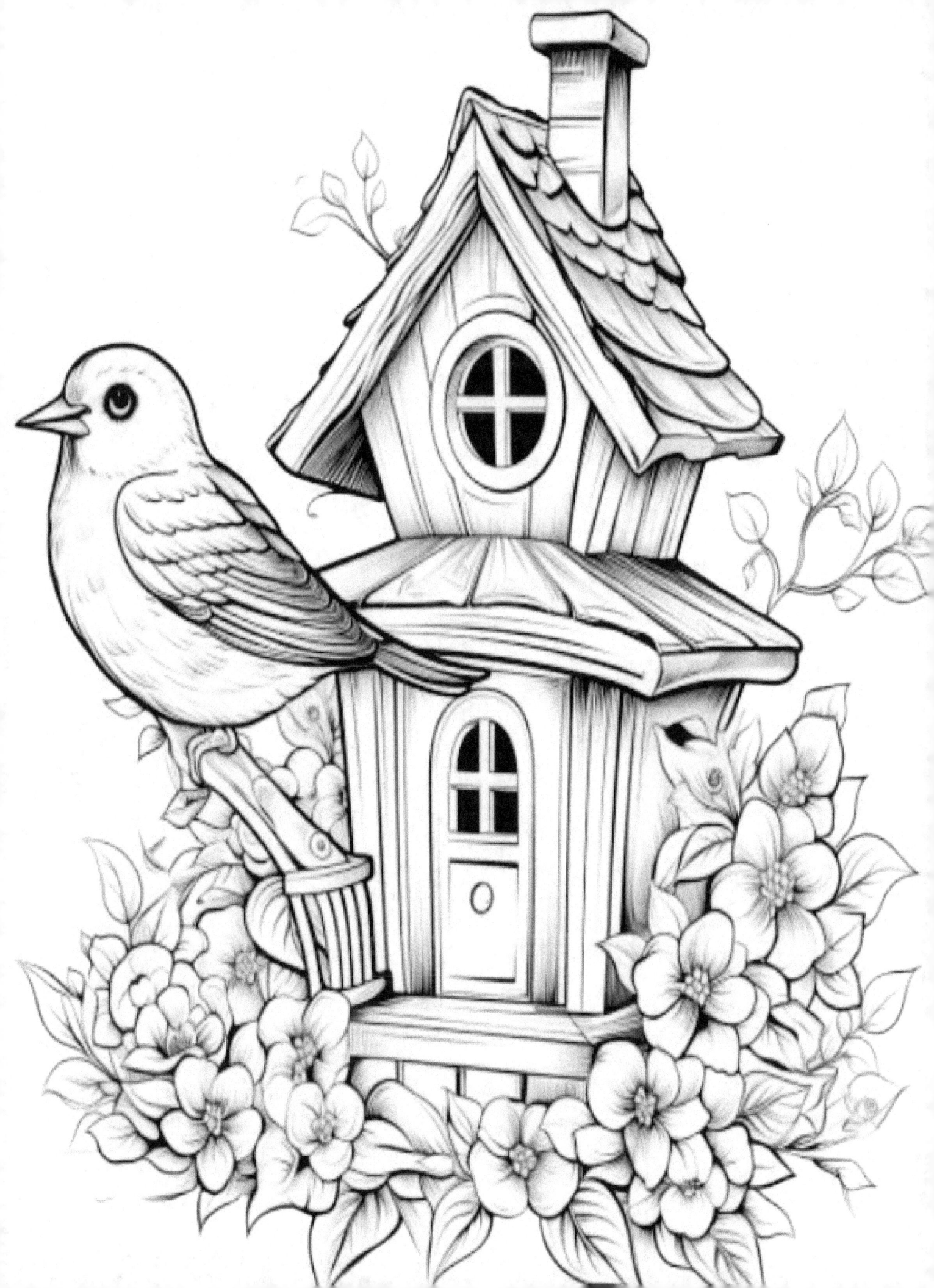

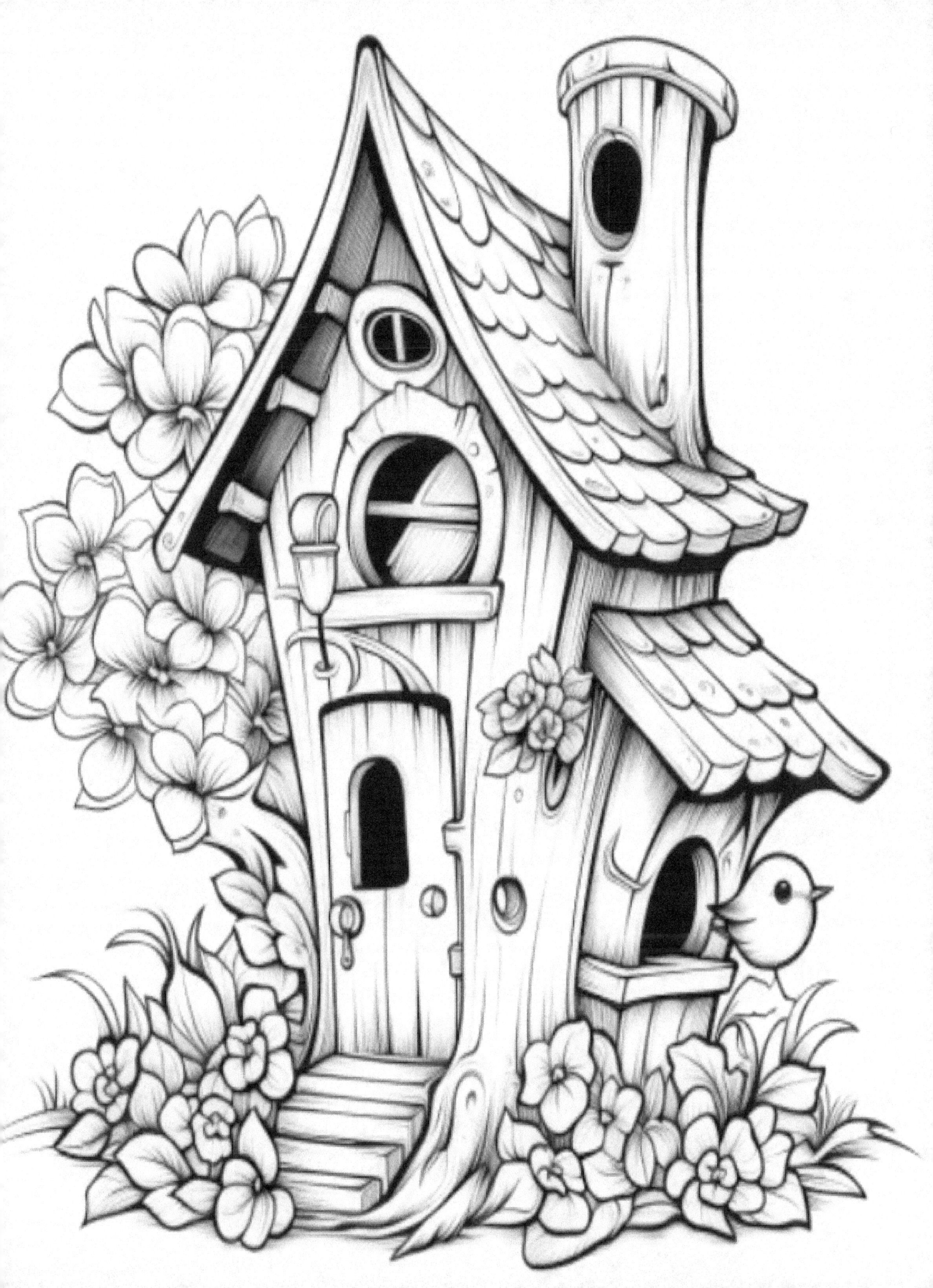

If you enjoyed this book, we ask that you kindly leave us an honest review. Your opinion matters to us and helps us improve our products!

We hope you enjoyed your coloring journey!

Below are some additional coloring books available through PKJ Publishing.

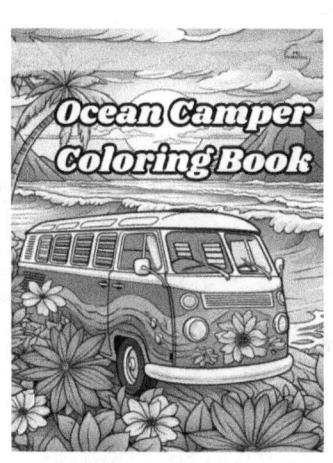
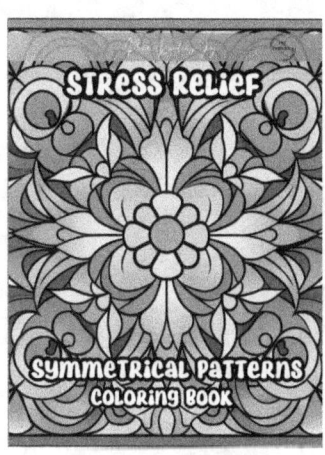
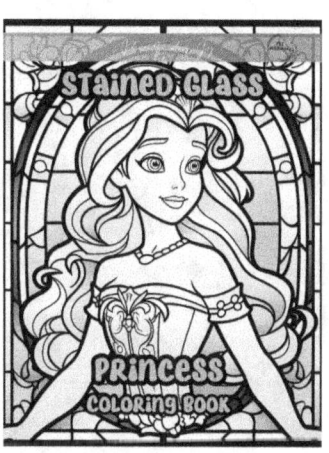

PKJ Facebook Page

PKJ Website

PKJ Amazon Books

PKJ Etsy Books

Be sure to share your beautiful creations on our Facebook page!